Praise For The

"In The Climb, John Rivera masterfully guides us through the essentials of leadership which every leader is wise to follow as they seek to climb to the mountain top of influence and impact. The insights John provides are both pragmatic and bedded on a solid biblical foundation. I encourage and highly recommend every leader to take a deep dive into the leadership high level principles The Climb provides."

Dr. Fernando Cabrera, LMHC, Ed.D.
Pastor and New York City Councilman

"Just as Abraham was blessed to be a blessing, John Rivera has been a great leader in the Christian community in Metro New York City over the last couple of decades. With his first book, The Climb, John gives young and seasoned leaders a practical, honest, and anointed path to godly success. With so much uncertainty in our world today, this devotional will help readers navigate their current circumstances and challenges with hope and courage and help inspire them to achieve new heights."

Tom Campisi, Publisher Tristate Voice
Metro New York's Christian News and Commentary

"John Rivera has walked through many open doors of ministry and leadership. In "The Climb," he shares some practical and inspirational lessons that can benefit both the early learner and the seasoned minister/leader. Whether in the Church, or the marketplace, leadership is a journey and in a uniquely warm way, John comes alongside his readers to assist in their climb."

"In The Climb, John Rivera skillfully & thoughtfully lays out what to do as a leader & what not to do. Using his own personal experience with transparency & vulnerability he urges us to take the path of authenticity, relying on the one who created us. Using my favorite scripture, Hebrews 6:10 "God is not unjust; He will not forget your work & the love you have shown Him as you have helped His people and continue to do so," John reminds us that we should never forget why we do what we do day after day year after year, and who we do it for. It's certainly worth the climb!"

"The Climb, by John Rivera is unequivocally a powerful leadership tool to navigate through ministry's toughest challenges. It contains experiences and strategies that are essential to fulfill your calling. It is a refreshing book for a tired heart in need of new strengths. A must read."

"John Rivera takes the reader by the hand on a revealing journey through the challenges and rewards of leadership. With the Bible as his truth compass, John combines practical, and personal experiences with eternal biblical truths to fully explain how an all-knowing God will equip those whom He calls, even when the called is seemingly unqualified. The Climb is a MUST HAVE in the resource library of anyone experiencing that awkward and uncomfortable, "who, me?" question, when challenged by the call to lead."

Rev. Lester Figueroa, Esq.
Calvary Assembly of God, NY

"John Rivera offers authentic and practical instruction based on the revelations he has received from God over his years of service to God and his people. The ability to use what is read *immediately* is what is attractive about The Climb. There are areas where you will say, "that's me," as we are all on a life journey. I especially enjoy the reflections that challenge the reader to find that personal application."

Arthur Higgins III MA, LPC, LCADC
Adjunct Faculty, Pillar College

"I salute my brother John Rivera for penning this thoughtful and well written book on leadership. John's ability to seamlessly merge scripture, humor, self-reflection, practical experiences, and relevant teaching stories from varied walks of life and cultures will hold the attention of novice and experienced leaders. His 4-2-1 analysis is worth the cost of the book. Leaders, young and seasoned, will deepen their leadership wisdom I.Q. by responding to reflection questions at the end of each chapter. It is clear the deeper you share, the higher you will climb."

Rev. Dr. Alfonso Wyatt, Founder
Strategic Destiny: Designing Futures Through Faith And Facts

"It only took one chapter of reading to realize that John Rivera has a real winning book on leadership with The Climb. With so many leadership books today leaning on secular principles, I love how John time and time again builds every leadership trait using wonderful biblical examples and spiritual illustrations. John's straightforward approach to leadership is a refreshing guide to being a spiritual leader in the chaotic culture in which we now live!"

Rev. Don James, Superintendent
New Jersey Ministry Network of the Assemblies of God

"I have heard John teach on leadership on multiple occasions. He teaches leadership principles based on personal experiences, and the realities of assisting others on their journey. That knowledge is communicated in 'The Climb' in very practical ways so that it is applicable to everyone, no matter where they may find them-selves in their leadership journey."

Rev. David Nuzzolo, CPA; JM
New York Ministry Network; Metro Executive Assistant

"Throughout the book The Climb, John Rivera's heart shines through as he challenges the reader to focus on God and not on others as they journey to become the leader God has created them to be. John uses many stories from the Bible as well as illustrations from today's world to challenge us to seek God's direction and rest in His faithfulness and beautiful plan for us."

Bev Zarges, Director of Fairs
NACCAP/Christian College Fairs

THE CLIMB

Practical Lessons For Today's Leader

JOHN RIVERA

Foreword by
REV. SAMUEL RODRIGUEZ

Library of Congress Control Number: TXU2-259-748

ISBN: 978-0-578-92193-8

Book Publishing Consultant: Sherylynne L. Rochester-Dix

Acknowledgement

First and foremost, I dedicate this book to my Lord and Savior Jesus Christ. Without Him, I would be lost and without purpose. I also dedicate this book to my wife Naomi and sons, Zachary and Matthew. Thank you for your love, daily inspiration, support and steady comedy relief. I love you so very much!

Last, but not least, I dedicate this book to every leader who wakes up each morning and decides to continue leading and serving even when there are no accolades, cameras, or millions of followers on social media. They simply do it for the love of God, the people they serve, and the call on their lives. I salute you; I celebrate you; and I believe that you will make a difference far beyond your wildest dreams. Stay the course!

"God is not unjust; he will not forget your work and the love you have shown him as you have helped his people and continue to help them."

Hebrews 6:10

Contents

Foreword

In an increasingly chaotic world, those of us who are in positions of leadership can often be tempted to quit. Phrases like, "It's too…" and "What if…?" play on a loop in our minds. Internal and external problems and pressures threaten to undo us. We see leaders fall publicly and we wonder, "Am I next?"

For many years, I have had the honor and privilege of serving in various leadership capacities: as a teacher, pastor, film producer, advisor to four U.S. presidential administrations and president of one of the largest organizations of Hispanic and Latino Christians in the world. While God has certainly given me a passion for leadership, there have been times in my life when I have thought, "Is this really worth it?"

The answer to that question is, of course, yes — because none of us ever lead on our own.

I could not do what I do every day without the grace and mercy of God, the love of my family and the support of my fellow leaders like John Rivera.

John and I met in Puerto Rico some years ago, and he impressed me as a man with a heart for God and for people. His enthusiasm for leading and empowering leaders was immediately evident. He is not afraid to tell the truth and poke a little fun at himself in the process. His heart is burdened for burned out leaders, and after the year we have experienced, I would say we have all been stretched to our breaking point.

The Climb is truly "for such a time as this." Through his devotional writings, John comes alongside us on our leadership journey, carrying us forward when we are tempted to stop and challenging us when we want to reverse course.

As John writes, "Don't give up on your dream and don't give up on your purpose. If you stay the course, and if you remain true to God, He will bless you and He will use you."

So grab your gear and let's get climbing.

Rev. Samuel Rodriguez
Lead Pastor, New Season Worship Center
President, National Hispanic Christian Leadership Conference
(NHCLC)
Author, "Survive to Thrive: Live a Holy, Healed, Healthy, Happy,
Humble, Hungry, and Honoring Life"

Introduction

"Somewhere between the bottom of the climb and the summit is the answer to the mystery why we climb."
— *Greg Child*

I love movies; especially those that make me laugh. Admittedly, I also enjoy watching a good tearjerker. Then there are those movies that achieve an array of emotions – those are my favorite. While I enjoy the emotional ride of some movies, there are movies that I simply remember because they carry a powerful message or lesson. One movie that fits that bill is undoubtedly *Apollo 13*.

This space-based docudrama has much to offer its audience, with its subtle tongue-in-cheek humor, intense drama and weighty interpersonal exchange in what ultimately becomes an unimaginable crisis. For those of you who have not watched it yet, I will also say that the story is rich in detail and cinematically captivating.

The film focuses on the three astronauts aboard Apollo 13 for NASA's fifth mission to the Moon. While on their momentous journey, an on-board explosion deprived the spacecraft of its most precious commodity - oxygen. To make matters worse, their electrical circuitry was compromised as well. The combination of these catastrophic events would ultimately force NASA's flight controllers to abort the Moon landing and turn the entire operation into a life-saving mission to get the three men home alive. This is when Gene Kranz, played by the incomparable Ed Harris, the flight director at NASA, rises to the top of his leadership game.

In *Apollo 13*, we see how Gene demonstrates stellar leadership responsiveness under great pressure and while facing unprecedented circumstances. Gene has many difficult decisions to make during an increasingly narrow window of opportunity. Most importantly, during all his decision-making, we witness his resolute drive to never succumb to defeat. Even though insurmountable odds shadow over Gene and his team, he is able to inspire everyone in that control room (and some of us in the audience).

Gene rallies his team, out of their customary modus operandi, and into a space that requires courage and determination. With each new, seemingly impossible situation, his response is simple, "we need to find a way to make it work." The confidence that resides within Gene is infectious and becomes the catalyst that unites this otherwise conventional team. He discovers ways to keep his team calm and focused on the task at hand, all while making his expectations crystal clear.

Apollo 13 demonstrates how a leader can coordinate a team effort to achieve a desired but unlikely result, as everyone plays his or her role in achieving a mutual goal. This is the reality that most leaders face daily on their personal leadership climb. Granted, most of us will not have to bring a crew back from outer space; however, we will likely face many decisions that impact the lives of others. The thing that makes this truth so daunting to many of us is that we must lead others in moments like this while leading ourselves to our personal leadership summit.

So, how long have you been climbing – two years, five, or twenty? Regardless of how long you have been climbing, we can all agree that "the climb" to our destiny is hard work. After a while, our leadership muscles become tired and it becomes harder to use them. Fatigue slows us down and we wonder if we will ever make it to the summit. Sometimes, we might even wonder if we were designed for the climb at all! I know that I've battled those questions more than once. I have considered the idea of giving up many times over the years; perhaps you have as well. And that is normal; after all, we are only human. Yet, despite those tired leadership muscles, and sore hands something within me has repeatedly said, "stay the course!"

I must say that I am grateful for the little voice that has kept me in the grind all these years. It's been hard work, but it has also been so rewarding to invest in the lives of business leaders and others in ministry throughout my days. Each time that I've walked away from a leadership encounter, it has felt as if a small piece of myself remained with that person. It is a special feeling that is at times difficult to articulate. However, there are few things that compare to the feeling of helping someone find meaning and success in their life's call.

As I mentioned before, each of us has a different "start-date" in our leadership journey, and each one looks quite different. Your unique climb will determine your experience, how you view the world around you and those whom you lead. I say this because of my own experience. It seems like yesterday, but I began this journey during my formative teen years. If I had a timeline in front of me, I could perhaps place a marker on key milestone experiences that fashioned the leader that I am today.

It was 1984, and I was only sixteen when I was thrust into my first leadership role. The youth director at the church that I attended was in his late 20's and exhausted after many years of leading our youth ministry. He approached me one Sunday afternoon to inform me that he could no longer lead the group. I immediately began to encourage him to not give up on us. He interrupted me and said, "Maybe you should take it over." I looked at him and chuckled. My response then, reminds me now, of Sarai's reaction when the Lord told her and Abram that they would have a miracle child in their old age. The Youth Director gazed back at me with an earnest look and said, "John, I am not kidding. I'm done and you are the only one who can take this ministry into the future."

I responded in protest with a trembling voice, "I'm too young. I can't lead the others; some of them are older than me." The age span represented in our youth group was broad. We had high school students (like myself), college students and several young professionals who were in their mid-twenties. I was convinced that they would never take me serious. He smiled and said, "Don't worry, I'll stand with you. You'll do a great job!"

Several weeks later, I was unanimously chosen by the youth group and Pastor to lead this motley group. Suffice it to say that I was both excited and overwhelmed by this sudden development.

Until this point, I was sure that my purpose was to be a drummer in a Christian band. Music was my life and that was all I wanted to do – nothing else had entered the equation. Music was my passion and my world. Few things mattered nearly as much as "jamming" with my fellow musicians. However, as I began to lead this group, my passions began to shift. I still loved music and few things were as enjoyable as singing, and playing the drums for my band (along with my childhood friends). Yet, something was blossoming within me, and I had no idea how it would forever transform the course of my life. I must confess that as I began to accept this burgeoning paradigm shift the metamorphic process felt uncanny and at times outright daunting! I want you to understand that I was at home behind my drum set. I could use my talent behind the "safe" canopy of my musical instrument – not to mention the other musicians who typically stood before me on stage. Yes, I could do my thing and remain "undetected."

Little did I know that I had begun leading from behind those drums. I was leading by influencing my band members' lives through a series of personal events, and even in small ways like the style of music we played and the arrangements that we incorporated into some of our original songs. I was developing into a leader and had no clue that I was growing! It is interesting to see how God will often begin a work in our lives, and we fail to perceive it until it is right in front of our faces! I was a leader and did not recognize it; at least not immediately.

To my surprise, this motley crew of teens and young adults almost immediately embraced my leadership and soon after, we began to see the Lord's favor over our ministry and lives. People, young and old, were inspired and excited about what the Lord was doing every Friday night.

Young people surrendered their lives to Jesus, as Savior and Lord. Even adults began to attend the Friday night youth services and eventually, attendance on Fridays matched that of Sundays! Was this a result of my leadership? In part, it was… but it was most definitely not entirely my doing. God was doing something special and powerful through the lives of young people who chose to believe for more. We became a team with a vision. We became a team with passion.

Shortly after my first year in leadership, we began a newsletter as a way of keeping teens engaged during the week. We also began to use this newsletter as a tool to invite friends and young family members to our Friday night services. There was a new passion for friendship evangelism in our group. That strategy hadn't previously existed in the history of our youth group.

Unchurched friends traditionally received invitations to the occasional evangelistic street rallies or special church services with the well-known evangelist from out of town. But now the young people became the evangelists; lives were being touched and some were being saved.

Even adults would approach me to say that they were going to bring a grandchild, nephew or niece to the Friday night services. You see this small group of young people was being used by God to bring about a form of revival that had not been experienced by this congregation in years.

So, we pressed on, refusing to settle for status quo. We applied our gifts and passions to a vision and made room for God to do what only He could do. It was an exciting season in my life. I learned the power of teamwork, vision and hope in the Lord. We began as a group of young people who simply attended the same church, enjoyed each other's company and social gatherings. We became a group of hard working, miracle believing, young people who dared to step outside of what was known as the "familiar place" of contentment. We became a team, unified by one vision and purpose.

Today, as I look back, I realize that this "success" was not based on my experience and talents... I had little or none to boast about at that early stage of my leadership journey. It was the presence and leadership of the Holy Spirit that made all the difference. We simply made room for Him. We depended on Him and believed in Him to do things above and beyond anything we had ever seen or experienced before.

Believe me, it was not all a bed of roses! I had to deal with many challenges. Not every young person embraced my leadership style or strategy, and resources were quite limited. Suffice it to say that church culture did not easily change in the 1980's. Nonetheless, the few years we spent together as a team became pivotal in our lives and even in the history of our small urban church. It was a great ride while it lasted, and that season became foundational to my journey.

Through this experience, I realized that God specializes in using the ones we least expect – I am living proof of that truth. During that season, I often looked up to God and repeated a statement like the words spoken by Gideon, "but how can I save Israel [*this youth group*]? My clan is the weakest in Manasseh [New York City], and I am the least in my family." (Judges 6:15)

This early stage of my leadership journey became the bedrock of my personal development. Today, I can look back and realize that I had an innate ability to lead my peers and even a number of adults. I had a passion and ability to take a vision and put legs on it for others to see, embrace and ultimately follow. There was growth and development in my leadership aptitude, and there was a leadership seed planted in my heart and mind that had been sown by God.

Today, I am the husband of a beautiful wife and father of two wonderful young men. I've been on my leadership journey for several decades now. At times, it has been a joyful and rewarding voyage. At other times, the pain has been too much to bear. Those painful moments have taught me how to rely on the everlasting and powerful arms of the Father.

With that said, both joyful and painful leadership experiences have served to provide me with countless tools that I use daily in my walk, as well as my work with other leaders (both fledgling and seasoned). Nothing goes to waste. Everything we experience can serve to elevate others and ourselves. We simply have to make a choice to learn every moment of every day as we climb toward our respective summits.

The many seasons that I have personally walked through, as well as the many experiences that my clients and ministry partners have experienced have become building blocks for growth and development. These lessons have led me to a place where I can now share this information with other leaders, pastors and even business heads beyond my immediate reach.

I must confess that I have grappled with the gnawing question: "why should I share this information in a book form? Why me Lord?" And the Lord has continued to impress on my heart that I am to speak to and encourage leaders wherever I go. God has done a unique thing in my life. It is not to be hoarded, hidden, or discarded; it is to be boldly shared.

I believe that the reasons for my role as a leader and mentor, and for this book are simple and clear— my journey, experience, education and most importantly relationship with Christ have positioned me to share His heart with leaders from a unique perspective.

Too often, the words from giants in a given field, while applicable, seem far beyond our reach because they have "arrived." They are the poster child for a particular category of ministry or business. These giants often enjoy millions of fans that follow their success or work via multiple platforms and websites. They lead ministries with multiple thousands in weekly attendance and for a lack of a better category; they are superstars in their own right.

I have no issues with ministries that enjoy vast audiences and are far reaching; they have their place and are part of the fabric of what God is doing in the world. But I will confess that during my early years of leadership, I became enamored with the image of a particular high-profile minister, so much so that I went as far as losing my identity for several years. I took my focus off the call God placed on my life and fixed my eyes on every move that this minister made. He had a big stage, and he also had my attention. I drifted into an imaginary world, daydreaming of being that person or at least a close facsimile. It became a trap that led to envy, self-doubt and a vicious cycle of frustration and unfulfilled ambition. My hope is that you don't fall into a similar trap or any thought cycle that delays your journey and growth as a leader.

We can easily excuse our inaction because the reality of reaching a certain level of success or impact simply seems too lofty and unrealistic.

That is why I believe God has chosen me to write a book of this kind. Consider me your fellow sojourner. I invite you to see me as someone who desires to do great things for God and who also desires to see you do likewise. So why not glean from my lessons learned during the last two decades, and apply them to your own journey? Take what I have and make it your own so that you may go back and apply it to your personal journey today. The things I will share in the following chapters will become germane to you today – there will be no need for you to "reach a certain level of aptitude or success."

I understand the realities of starting a small ministry and business and I understand the challenges of achieving things for the Lord with few resources. I know what it means to fail and desperately reach up to grab God's hand so that I may get back in the boat and start the process all over again. In other words, I understand the importance of complete reliance on God. After all, He is the true leader in our leadership journey. In short, this book is not about building your own kingdom or resume. It is not about building a mega ministry or church. It is, however, about building His kingdom, growing as a leader and shining the greatest possible light on His name, for His glory.

Perhaps you are starting your ministry or business today. Perhaps you are the leader of a church or ministry with 1,000 or more followers – I believe that the lessons contained in the following pages can and will help you grow and refine your outlook as a leader. I also believe it will help those who lead alongside you today.

"For when one says, "I follow Paul," and another, "I follow Apollos," are you not mere human beings? What, after all, is Apollos? And what is Paul? Only

servants, through whom you came to believe—as the
Lord has assigned to each his task. I planted the seed,
Apollos watered it, but God has been making it grow.
So neither the one who plants nor the one who waters is
anything, but only God, who makes things grow. The
one who plants and the one who waters have one
purpose, and they will each be rewarded according to
their own labor. For we are co-workers in God's service;
you are God's field, God's building."

- 1 Corinthians 3:4-9

In this book, I will share devotional messages that I trust will both challenge and inspire you onto greater "leadership exploits;" especially as we navigate through this new and daunting paradigm before us. COVID-19, civil unrest, and global tumults have all impacted how we see the world and how we lead – but one thing has not been affected, nor changed. The truths found in Scripture remain as true and relevant today as they did the day they were first inspired by God.

What you are about to read comes from the halls of my own leadership journey. It is a compilation of my leadership teachings, journal entries and personal devotionals that grew out of times of great victories and some really tough moments. This is an intimate endeavor that God has chosen to make public. I am living-out my life for the cause of the Kingdom of God.

I desire to see God's people find their purpose, live out that devotion to the fullest, and impact the world in ways far beyond their greatest dreams and aspirations. I want to see those called to leadership, wholeheartedly embrace their purpose and lead in excellence. I hope to eliminate some of the excuses that have held you back long enough – it is now time to touch the world!

I am aware of the fact that many leaders have already begun their "exit strategy" because of all that we have experienced in our world since 2020. I would urge you to scrap that exit plan and to once again embrace all that God has for you today and into the future. Leaders have become a priceless commodity in this climate. You are invaluable! Don't give up on your dream and don't give up on your purpose. If you stay the course, and if you remain true to God, He will bless you and He will use you.

May I also challenge you to go beyond reading words on pages? Use this opportunity to climb the mountain before you. As you climb you will discover the God you serve and the leader you are meant to be in this life – and yes, even in this new world where we are actively trying to define "normal." Climb in confidence, knowing that your life will forever change, as well as the lives of those whom you lead. Allow the principles found in this book to penetrate both heart and mind. Invite the Lord each time you sit to read through these pages. I believe that you will hear His voice instructing you in the way that you should go. Take moments to meditate and ask Him questions about your own leadership journey. As you do this, He will speak and He will show you great things that will set the stage for a better tomorrow.

With that in mind, I have included several questions at the end of each chapter. They are there to help you reflect on your life's purpose and where you are today in light of your calling. Use this space to enter your thoughts about what God is saying to you through each page of this book. But don't limit yourself to the Q&A sections; use any page you wish to enter your notes and reflections. This book should become a tool. Remember to place a date next to your notes, so that you can return to these pages and reflect on your own journey in the years ahead.

Every leader on your team should embrace a similar challenge so that you may all climb to that next tier of leadership and intimacy with Christ. He is calling you to the summit. Can you hear His voice? Are you still afraid and concerned about your ability to lead in this climate? Take this Scripture to heart and let's start to climb:

> *"Don't worry about anything; instead, pray about*
> *everything; tell God your needs, and don't forget to*
> *thank him for his answers. If you do this, you will*
> *experience God's peace, which is far more wonderful*
> *than the human mind can understand. His peace will*
> *keep your thoughts and your hearts quiet and at rest as*
> *you trust in Christ Jesus."*

- Philippians 4:6-7

I look forward to hearing many testimonies about God's work in your lives as you make the conscience decision to climb to greater altitudes and adventures with Jesus. The following verse is an essential part of your mountaineering gear as you begin *The Climb:*

> *"Do not conform to the pattern of this world, but be*
> *transformed by the renewing of your mind. Then you*
> *will be able to test and approve what God's will is —*
> *His good, pleasing and perfect will."*

- Romans 12:2

4-2-1 The Path Toward Genuine Leadership

"In our abandonment we give ourselves over to God just as God gave Himself for us, without any calculations. The consequences of abandonment never enter into our outlook because our life is taken up in Him."
— Oswald Chambers

During my early days in leadership, I searched tirelessly for the proverbial magic pill that would position me at the head of the line. I imitated leaders who I admired, and subscribed to seemingly supernatural strategies that ultimately proved to be replete with mindless gimmicks. Thankfully, I quickly arrived at a similar conclusion as King Solomon did in Ecclesiastes 2:11, "Yet when I surveyed all that my hands had done and what I had toiled to achieve, everything was meaningless, a chasing after the wind; nothing was gained under the sun."

Today, I am thankful for that season of seeking authenticity and truth in my personal journey as a leader. It was at this point of realization that I began to recognize who I was as a leader, and the importance of finding an intimate place and function in God's master plan. This revelation took place when I approached God as my authentic self – John Rivera, the one who He called to His service.

My desire is that you will discover ideas that will compel you to move into a place of personal transformation. I can confidently say that you will encounter God's Word and His compass for you. I use the word "compass" because God will rarely give you detailed "step-by-step" GPS directions: "At the next light, make a left, then stay in the right lane…" He will most likely give you directions that resemble a compass. Ever wonder why He does that?

It's simple, but not easy. God always endeavors to grow your faith as He leads you in this journey. He is continually growing us and purging everything that is impure or resembles extra baggage. This takes time, hard work and complete surrender. Truth be told, that is counterintuitive to the typical 21st century leader who desires precooked and prepackaged results.

We rely so much on data, charts, and calculations and let's not forget our committees of experts and social media specialists before we make any decision. Not so on this journey of faith and renewal. You will only need a yielded heart, an internal compass and one foot moving in front of the other. This will be an old-school experience.

Most of us must face the daily pressure that is created by the constant bombardment of social media engines that promote a growing genre of "Super-Pastors" and "Leadership Experts." As I said before, I have wasted far too much time comparing and fantasizing what it would be like if I were this guy or the other. These folks seemingly have the market cornered on success, and we wake up every day and try to figure out how we can become the next: *fill in the blank.*

I am sure that if I were standing before you this very moment, you could fill-in that blank with at least 5 names of people you aspire to emulate. While there is nothing intrinsically wrong with admiring and learning from successful leaders, it cannot be your singular driving force. It is a dangerous practice, as it resides far too close to idolatry. You might say, "Hey John, are you taking this a bit too far?"

Um… No. If we are honest, we often find ourselves running to blogs, books and sermons created by these "super-humans" before running to the Lord in prayer or Scripture. Truth be told, we have all been there, but now is the time to face the truth of our dependence on man's wisdom. It's time to repent, and to move on with the Lord's counsel. Man cannot be our principal source! God can use man to bring about His message and voice, but we must always understand that God is the true source of all wisdom and direction for us as leaders and more importantly as Christians. This message is effectively offered in Jeremiah 17:5-6 (AMP),

"…Cursed is the man who trusts in and relies on mankind, making [weak, faulty human] flesh his strength, and whose mind and heart turn away from the Lord."

Remember this, "**imitation fosters limitation.**" It will keep you from the best version of who you were created to be in this life. Striving for bigger things in life and leadership is a wonderful thing, but striving to be like another minister or leader, whether consciously or unconsciously, is never a good thing; imitations are never as good as the real thing, so use your time and gifts wisely.

Now, we have all learned from others, gleaned from great leaders and we may from time to time borrow ideas or quotes. You will notice that I use quotes in this book from people whom I respect. The key here is to avoid complete reliance on man for every word, thought and decision.

Leaders must enter the place of complete and sacrificial surrender and obedience as a party of one. It is a place where prominent pastors and leaders are unable to feed you great one-liners and where your own team is unable to accompany you. It is the place of intimate "shedding and stripping," where only you and God can convene. It is unfortunately also the place where many stop or fall off altogether, right before they reach that proverbial mountaintop. Don't allow this process and the accompanying discomfort to keep you from experiencing God's best for you. You must press on and climb up.

We must move away from kneejerk leadership reactions that are devoid of God's input and presence. But rather, we must incorporate a practice of regularly consulting with Jesus. He alone will lead us and show us the heart of the Father as it relates to our journey and maturity as leaders and servants.

Fair warning: The information ahead will stretch you and will push the boundaries of where you have been prior to this moment in time.

Are you ready? I believe you are! As a matter of fact, I would like to ask you to do something unusual. Take a pen and underline my "fair warning" above and write today's date next to it – then place your initials next to it. Go ahead. I'll wait… I want that statement to become your personal contract and commitment to going beyond what you have done in the past. If you are going to do this, then make it count.

4-2-1

I discovered the 4-2-1 principle while reading Abraham's story in Genesis chapter 22. Interestingly enough, I read this chapter as I prepared to teach a Sunday school class to a wonderful group of teens at my home church. It took on a life of its own as I prepared and even as I shared the principles with the class. The simple life lesson quickly evolved into one of my favorite leadership lessons in the ensuing months. Since then, I've shared this lesson at leadership conferences and with individual leaders, and now I will share it with you.

4-2-1 is the process by which you reach that place of clear purpose and intimacy with God. It is that place where you can show yourself faithful to accomplish your God-ordained mission and bring your team to that next level. Now, while this topic is largely a spiritual principle, it also carries great practical implications that can be applied to your everyday leadership journey. We can touch on that further toward the latter part of this chapter.

Now, take some time to first read through Genesis 22. As you read, allow the Holy Spirit to open your heart and mind. Here we go!

> *"Some time later God tested Abraham. He said to him, "Abraham!" "Here I am," he replied. Then God said, "Take your son, your only son, whom you love—Isaac —and go to the region of Moriah. Sacrifice him there as a burnt offering on a mountain I will show you." Early the next morning Abraham got up and loaded his donkey. He took with him two of his servants and his son Isaac. When he had cut enough wood for the burnt offering, he set out for the place God had told him about. On the third day Abraham looked up and saw the place in the distance. He said to his servants, "Stay here with the donkey while I and the boy go over there. We will worship and then we will come back to you." Abraham took the wood for the burnt offering and placed it on his son Isaac, and he himself carried the fire and the knife. As the two of them went on together, Isaac spoke up and said to his father Abraham, "Father?" "Yes, my son?" Abraham replied. "The fire and wood are here," Isaac*

*said, "but where is the lamb for the burnt offering?"
Abraham answered, "God himself will provide the
lamb for the burnt offering, my son." And the two of
them went on together. When they reached the place God
had told him about, Abraham built an altar there and
arranged the wood on it. He bound his son Isaac and
laid him on the altar, on top of the wood. Then he
reached out his hand and took the knife to slay his son.
But the angel of the Lord called out to him from heaven,
"Abraham! Abraham!" "Here I am," he replied. "Do
not lay a hand on the boy," he said. "Do not do
anything to him. Now I know that you fear God,
because you have not withheld from me your son, your
only son." Abraham looked up and there in a thicket he
saw a ram caught by its horns. He went over and took
the ram and sacrificed it as a burnt offering instead of
his son. So Abraham called that place The Lord Will
Provide. And to this day it is said, "On the mountain
of the Lord it will be provided." The angel of the Lord
called to Abraham from heaven a second time and said,
"I swear by myself, declares the Lord, that because you
have done this and have not withheld your son, your
only son, I will surely bless you and make your
descendants as numerous as the stars in the sky and as
the sand on the seashore. Your descendants will take
possession of the cities of their enemies, and through
your offspring all nations on earth will be blessed,
because you have obeyed me."*

Genesis 22:1-18

What a powerful story! Now let's dissect this further and review the highlights of what you just read:

- God invites Abraham into a sacrificial journey (Isaac was to die).
- Abraham immediately responds and acts upon God's request (no evidence of vacillation).
- Abraham builds a team which included two servants, his son and of course himself.
- They gathered required transport, resources and tools for the journey ahead and departed.
- They stop – Abraham instructs his servants to wait there until he and Isaac return.
- Abraham and Isaac carry on, and there is a weighty conversation about "missing items" required for the sacrifice.
- They reach the mountaintop – the destination prescribed by God Himself.
- Abraham builds the altar and lays his son on top.
- Moment of truth – sacrifice is about to occur; Abraham raises knife.
- God intervenes and demonstrates His character, and the purpose behind the journey to the mountaintop.
- God sets the stage for Abraham and Isaac to move onto higher ground as leaders of their clan, and for generations to follow!

Some of you might be thinking about all this right now and are wondering, "Where is the leadership concept and what do the numbers 4, 2, and 1 have to do with this story?" I am glad you asked! Continue to read and we will begin to explore this concept.

4- Abraham & Company

We must first revisit the beginning of this story… God speaks to Abraham, provides instructions and Abraham jumps into action:

> *³ Early the next morning Abraham got up and loaded his donkey. He took with him two of his servants and his son Isaac.*

As you can see, this journey began with a team of four: Abraham, Isaac and two servants. This is where we arrive at our first number in the 4-2-1 principal: 4. Let us examine this further. Each of the 4 men had a clear mission, responsibility, and role on this team. All players had a critical role to contribute to this expedition, especially during the early leg of their journey. The two servants were there to help resource the material, organize and place items on the transport animal and remain available to Abraham throughout the journey. They were to assist their leader, Abraham, with any and all requests that would ensure a successful trip and eventual return to their camp.

Keep in mind that this journey was not a few blocks down a paved road with several diners and coffee shops on the way. It is clear from the context of this story that Abraham, Isaac and the two servants began their journey at Beer-sheba, and the narrative records that "on the third day" Abraham saw their destination in the distance. Since 2 Chronicles 3:1 identifies the temple mount in Jerusalem as "Mount Moriah," it appears that Jerusalem was their intended destination.[1] This would have been a journey of approximately 30 – 40 miles through desolate terrain and extreme weather: scorching heat during the day and frigid temperatures during nightfall hours.

We can safely conclude that these men had to take on many tasks each day to ensure that they would arrive safely and more importantly, alive. I am sure that they had to set-up and break-down camp, cook, and so much more. This was most certainly not a stroll in the park.

This portion of the story reminds me of the realities that most leaders encounter when we hear the voice of God calling us into the next leg of our journey. That might be a call to launch a new church, ministry or perhaps a business venture. If you already have that in place, your call may be to expand your reach to a broader community of those whom you believe God has called you to touch. If you are a business owner, perhaps you are now exploring a missional element that you believe must become part of your plan, and that first step now awaits you.

Sometimes, the call is to a cleaning out of old ways and failed practices that are drenched in man's way of doing things. God will often call you out of the ordinary and into a place of complete reliance on the supernatural or His mysterious ways.

One thing that I have learned is that God will use people to partner with you and to grow your God-given vision into reality. This is the time when you as a leader, must seek His face and ask for direction about the people who should join you on this journey.

Though the story found in Genesis 22 does not go into Abraham's selection process of the two men, I am confident that he knew exactly whom he would consider. As Abraham embraced God's call to this trip, I can imagine him thinking through his selection: "I need two men; one who is skilled in wilderness travel, another who knows how to cook and handle essential duties for survival…"

Again, that is my imagination, but it makes sense, right? What are the skills and gifts that will be required for this next leg of your journey? What are the spiritual attributes that will become essential? As you begin to prepare and plan, God will be faithful to bring the right people in, and He will align your hearts in ways that are far beyond your ability. To successfully experience this, you must also allow yourself to connect with people and observe their gifts and skills. You will need to understand their hearts and aspirations, and most importantly,

how all these vital assets support the weight of God's vision
for you.

I remember meeting a pastor some years ago. He relocated
his entire family from Australia in response to the call of God on
his life. What was that call? He was to launch a church in the
heart of New York City. They had no friends or family in the city,
so they simply began with family devotionals in a park located
near their neighborhood. Over time, they began to meet other
families in their community and extended invitations to join them
in the park. This is where their journey began to take shape. This
is also when the initial players joined their loosely formed team.

Several months down the road, there were enough folks gathering so that the young pastor saw the need to launch their first
monthly home gathering as a church. Little by little they began to
meet musicians and volunteers who were both talented and available to join them.

My favorite story was of a "chance meeting" between this
pastor, his wife and the waiter at a local café that they frequented.
As their waiter tended to the couple one day, the conversation
about ministry came up and the pastor mentioned, "At this point
everything is in place for our first official service… all we need is
a drummer."

To their amazement, the waiter that they knew for quite some
time by then mentioned, "I'm a drummer and I'd love to help."
The waiter eventually became a vital part of that young pastor's
team. Only God can orchestrate such a sweet and miraculous
event.

Today, this couple is leading a multi-campus church in New
York City, and they recently branched out into the New York tri-
state area and even into other countries. They are touching thousands of lives every week.

They needed a team and the Lord provided. While some of
the folks who started with this couple remain to this day, not
everyone became a permanent fixture of this ministry. Some

remained for a season and moved on, and that is a reality that you must accept as you move forward in your 4-2-1 journey.

There will inevitably be times when God will call you or members of your team to move on from a given place of relationship. This happens so that we are able to release our dependence on man and reengage with God. It positions us to receive new or greater marching orders. This is also how God will provide the team that is most appropriate for each level and season of your journey. The reality of essential team members leaving your side will rattle your cage or any leader for that matter. However, we must understand and accept that it is part of God's design. Not everyone is called to every stage and level of "your" journey. It is necessary that you genuinely grasp this truth. It is also an important lesson for those who will join you. Remember this, they too are on their own 4-2-1 journeys.

As you move forward you will need to remain attune to God's voice. For some of us, losing key team members may stir-up emotions of abandonment and distrust. Some of us might have been raised in a home where a parent or sibling may have abandoned us. As a result, losing people becomes a challenging part of life. Some of us might encounter the loss of a business partner or ministry leader, leaving you wondering whom you can trust. You see, some folks may leave for the wrong reasons and it may cause you pain. Or perhaps an unexpected death claims a team member and carrying on through the grief seems too much to stomach. Another may have to move for work reasons but the timing couldn't be worse for your ministry. Unfortunately, the mess left behind may set you back or the leader/partner may have left a trail of bodies behind him or her.

These experiences will require your immediate attention and leadership. This is not the time for avoidance and procrastination. In other words, don't ignore it or brush it under the rug. Face it. Explain it to your team and repair it – if necessary. Once you do this, you are positioned to move forward.

The good news is that God is never caught off guard. He takes the impromptu and sometimes careless decisions of some team members and weaves those very things into his master plan – for your good and His glory. This helps us to remain in step with Him. It also helps your team to see that God is ultimately in control – not the departing team member. Conversely, some team members will leave with great honor and dignity. They will leave things better than when they arrived and will leave a team behind overflowing in vision and inspiration for the future. Those are the leaders who are most difficult to release.

Whether it is a good or less than ideal separation, never use the event to vent or pour-on a guilt trip. Use the opportunity to celebrate God's faithfulness and the beauty of His master plan. This is also your platform to remind those who remain, that a breathing and living purpose remains before you as a team.

Take a time to pray over your departing team member as part of your separation process. Depending on the unique circumstances of that relationship, you may want to do this in private. Under ideal conditions, this should be done as a shared team "send-off." Most importantly, when the Lord releases a member of your team, do not get in the way. He knows best.

2- Abraham and Isaac

As we read in Scripture, Abraham leaves his two servants behind at a given point of their journey. As mentioned earlier, not everyone is intended to be a companion throughout your entire leadership journey. Agreed? Some folks will enter your journey with a unique set of skills and experience that will serve you ideally during a given season. Likewise, you may become instrumental in the lives of those who choose to serve you and your ministry. God has a way of weaving our lives together at the right time for maximum return and glory to His name. He is an amazing conductor of our symphonic lives. *The lesson here is simple: Not everyone who is key (or important to you) is kin to you.*

The work and design over your leadership life is one-of-a-kind. There will be things that only you can do. There will be places where you must go alone or with a select group of people. Only God can determine who goes where and when. This requires that we become adept at listening to His voice and the instructions that will keep us moving toward the appropriate trajectory.

At this juncture in their story, father & son continue their journey to the top of the mountain, while the two servants wait behind and it is then that Abram and Isaac have a heartfelt and intimate conversation.

Those who will play a more intimate and strategic role in your leadership journey will be the ones who move beyond the crowd and into the inner workings of God's plan for you, your ministry or your business. There may also be many other players performing vital roles. Don't be mistaken, you will need the entire team; however, you may have a group that will be picked by God and revealed to you for a distinctive work. This is the soil from which future leaders may emerge to carry the vision beyond you. These are the people who can be entrusted with your heart, vision and the intimacy of true partnership. This requires trust and vulnerability at a level that most people will avoid. But not you! You know that it is worth the risk and worth the hard work.

I just used the dreaded "R" word: risk. Whenever you choose to work with another living and breathing person, there is an inherent risk. No one is perfect, and every person you bring along with you has the potential for failure, or even betrayal. That is exactly why we must keep Christ at the center of this journey and experience. He will mitigate the risk and protect you in the process.

If you recall, Jesus chose an improbable group of men to join Him on a special journey over a period of three years. Some grew, some gave Him a tough time, and one betrayed Him. However, none surprised Him or the Father. None fell through the cracks and spoiled God's plan. God promises the same to you and me. Trust God in this process. Prayerfully choose the people who will walk with you in this stage of your passage. Trust God with your choices.

Remember this, *"He will make all things work out for the good of those who love him and are called according to His purpose."* [2]

In the case of Abraham's story, God gave him only one choice for this second leg of the journey: Isaac. This is where Abraham's mandate and vision were shared with Isaac. During this leg of the journey, the two were able to have conversations that might not have occurred in the company of the other two men. There might have been tears, intimate questions and dialogue that only came to fruition during this critical stage of their climb.

While the Bible doesn't give much detail about the dialogue between Abraham and Isaac, we do see that the son asked about missing key elements of the sacrifice. This topic must have been a central theme during the conversations between the two. As a father, Abraham assured his son that the Lord would provide: *"God himself will provide the lamb for the burnt offering, my son." And the two of them went on together."* [3]

I love the fact that the NIV uses the word "together." In Hebrew, the word "together" is *yachad*, which means, "to be one," or "united." That is powerful imagery. The Lord knew that in order for the mountain top experience to be optimal, Abraham and Isaac had to be united, or one in spirit, mind and purpose. This leg of their journey made that possible.

As a leader, this is what you will need with your team, but much more so with those in your inner circle. If there is any fiber of disunity in your core, then you will be greatly compromised. It will only be a matter of time before it rears its ugly head. You may not see it now, after a year or even after five, but rest assured, you will see it, and you will feel it. As you pray, and build your team, ask the Lord for "yachad."

As you promote and protect unity in your inner circle, you will experience a power and energy unlike anything else in the context of organizational life. This will invigorate your entire team and it will even reach those outside of your inner circle. Now that is exciting! I will elaborate more about that later in this chapter.

If you are struggling with this concept because you want to treat everyone equally or you don't want to offend any team member, I would urge you to consider the fact that even Jesus employed this same model. For example, He had the 70 disciples, and 12 Apostles but then there were the three who represented His inner circle: Peter, James and John (Matthew 17:1). Each group played a unique role and was seamlessly aligned, with the nuances of Jesus' plan for humanity.

However, the final three men on this list experienced things the others were not designated to witness. This did not diminish the value of the others; after all, Jesus did call his Disciples "friends." (see John 15:15) But He did elevate the three to a place of honor and distinction. All these groups formed the very orchestra that God used to play His symphony of love that was ultimately performed on the cross by His son Jesus.

The grand finale of this performance took place on the third day, when Jesus returned from the grave to give us access to the Father. While on earth, he also reunited with His team. No one was excluded.

1- Abraham

We just discussed the importance and value of the inner circle, but keep in mind that there will always be things that only the leader can do and places where only you (the leader) may go. No one else may accompany you. I'll say it again, no one else –

as designed by God! While Isaac did reach the final stop of this journey alongside his father, it was Abraham's responsibility to build the altar and offer the sacrifice.

I must pause here to make it absolutely clear that Isaac's role was pivotal to this entire story. Without him, there would have been no potential for the "sacrifice." Yet, this portion of the journey was a call to Abraham and a test of his faith and commitment to the purpose over his life. Notwithstanding, there was a similar call to faith over Isaac, but for the purpose of this chapter, we will consider and focus on our good friend Abraham.

When Abraham arrived at the top of the mountain, he proceeded to build the altar and then made the decision to move ahead with what would be one of the most difficult tasks in his life. He bound his son and laid him on the altar to be sacrificed. As he, in faith, raised the knife above his head, God spoke, "Abraham!" The Lord intervened, provided a sacrifice[4] and the rest, as we say – is history.

We can agree, that Abraham's act of obedience allowed him to not only grow in his faith, but also in his understanding of God's heart. He realized that God never intended to accept the sacrifice of Isaac. He used this journey and moment to reveal His heart as Abba Father to Abraham. He showed Abraham that He was a God of grace, one who would provide at the right time, the perfect sacrifice. God demonstrated to Abraham that He was unlike any other god known to man before this moment in time. In short, Abraham's paradigm and perspective on God was absolutely transformed by this experience.

Had Abraham refused this invitation to the mountaintop, he would have never met God in this manner. He might have eventually encountered this attribute of God down the road. But he would have robbed himself of a blessing and a greater level of intimacy with the Lord. This too is the risk that we as leaders take when we vacillate upon receipt of an invitation to ascend. Granted, these invitations are intimidating at times (most of the time, actually). Yet, without those moments, we become ill equipped to lead and to fulfill the purpose before us.

Have you received invitations from the Lord to ascend and experience Him at a greater level? Have you accepted the invitation, even if a sacrifice is to be involved in the process? How long would it take for you to respond with an affirmative, "yes" if the invitation arrived today?

If you are at a crossroads where the invitation to the mountaintop has been issued, but you are frozen by fear or intimidation, choose today to take that next step. Choose this very moment to say "yes" to this higher call on your leadership journey.

In fact, why don't you take a moment now to lay this book aside and spend some time with the Lord in prayer? Tell Him that you accept His call to the mountaintop. Receive this moment as a reminder that His plans for you are great. Get in step with your Heavenly Father. You will never regret this choice.

As it was for Abraham and his journey to the mountaintop, no one else can construct the alter God has asked you to build and upon which to present a sacrifice. There are things in the leadership journey that only you can do. They absolutely cannot be delegated to "the team." If you attempt to delegate your task or journey to another team member, you will secure failure for your team and most definitely for yourself. At this crucible, you will encounter one of the most critical moments as a leader.

If God has chosen you to engage in the stage called "**1**," and to meet Him at the altar of sacrifice on the mountaintop, then it is you who must ascend. You may consult with your team, ask for prayer or even meet with your mentor. That is fine and well, but the decision to carry on is one that will absolutely alter your future and give you a perspective that is only realized at the top of the mountain. You will never see the same terrain from ground level.

This is the final stage of the stripping process. It is what defines you as a leader. This final stage is where you receive your next order, and it determines the impact you can offer to those whom you serve and those who serve alongside you. So, rise up! Be courageous and experience the transformative power of this call.

Applying this principle will require a certain level of intimacy with God that will only come as a result of time well spent with the Father. *As you draw near to your God, He will draw near to you* and those who follow your lead will also be challenged and stirred toward their own unique leadership journey. The person who loves the process has a much greater chance of success than the person who simply loves the outcome. Embrace the process and experience great results!

Practical Organizational Application

So, wait a minute John! You're saying that this concept of 4-2-1 can also help a business owner or the leader of an organization who is in the process of fine-tuning his strategy?

Yes, it can!

Here is a simple truth: a mass movement rarely begins with the masses, but with a few passionate and driven people who compel many others to action. That is why more and more organizations realize that to grow in size and impact, they must first grow small: 4-2-1. Individuals and small teams can achieve goals, return to the larger group and influence the masses with new vision, solutions, etc. Fine-tuning and sharpening is how organizations weather the changing times, while staying true to vision and purpose. Following are a few ideas for you to consider:

1. **Small groups are agile:** Generally speaking, the fewer people you have in a group, the easier it is to rally the team and realize consensus. That's because

meetings don't need to be postponed multiple times to accommodate conflicting schedules. You also don't need to waste time bringing everyone up to speed on new developments over and over again. Lastly, there tend to be fewer disagreements and misunderstandings in smaller groups.

2. **Small groups stimulate solidarity:** When there are fewer people on a team, it is much easier to get to know one another and become comfortable sharing ideas. Remember, ideas can at times be considered a risk. So, it takes courage and trust to voice ideas – especially those that are outside the box. Many churches have embraced the concept of "small groups" for this very reason. It promotes community, creativity and open dialogue.

3. **Smaller groups promote unity:** With smaller numbers, individuals are far likelier to come to the assistance of another group member. If the mission is important enough, they'll even be willing to pay the price for the group. This idea is most evident in elite military groups. Over time, they become like family.

4. **Small groups can become more focused:** It's quite difficult and time-consuming to bring a large group of people around a focused and time sensitive task. You will always be more productive using fewer people as you create a streamlined process. The question that a leader must ask here is, "do we want to be a laser or a flood light?" They are both sources of light, but the focused beam of the laser can also cut through all sorts of matter.

5. **Small groups expend fewer human resources:** When you have an unwieldy number of people on a team, chances are that a significant number of them are not actively contributing. They're actually

disappearing in the sea of people, wasting time that could be much better spent on other projects. When you whittle teams down to a lesser core group, you help ensure that everyone is using their time and energy more productively.

6. **Smaller groups foster mentoring:** Even in smaller teams, it's likely that members will have different backgrounds, and areas of know-how. In fact, these groups present a great opportunity for seasoned people to coach less experienced members. This is good for a young organization because you're developing junior people without spending additional resources.

REFLECTION

The 4-2-1 Process seems to be one that expresses how God systematically strips the leader of dependence on "man" and fosters a one-on-one experience with God. Can you give examples of **other leaders in the Bible** who shared similar experiences? How does their story relate to you?

_____

_____

_____

_____

_____

_____

_____

_____

_____

_____

_____

Where do you currently find yourself as it relates to the 4-2-1-Process? What's your next step?

_____

_____

_____

_____

_____

_____

_____

_____

Can you elaborate on how this process of "reduction" and "fine-tuning" can also be applied practically in your own organizational setting - what might be the short-term benefits?

_____

_____

_____

_____

_____

_____

_____

_____

_____

_____

_____

_____

_____

_____

_____

_____

_____

_____

_____

1. "Matthew Henry Complete Bible Commentary Online." *Bible Study Tools*, Salem Web Network, www.biblestudytools.com/commentaries/matthew-henry-complete
2. Romans 8:28
3. Genesis 22:8 NIV
4. Genesis 22:13

2

Con Games

"We are all faced with a series of great opportunities brilliantly disguised as impossible situations."
— Charles R. Swindoll

What do you think when you hear the words, "con game?" Do you think of mob movies? Perhaps you think of crooked characters from some television show or novel? We all have our own concept of a con, but let's start by exploring a definition and context that will help us grow as leaders in a very important area. So, what is a con game? Here is how Webster's Dictionary defines it:

> *confidence game (n).- a swindle in which the swindler, after gaining the victim's confidence, robs the victim by cheating at a gambling game,*

appropriating funds entrusted for investment, or the like. Also called, con fidence trick.

Here we find a weapon often used by the enemy to push us off track, delay and ultimately halt our forward progress. He may not consider bringing you or me to a place of moral defeat because he knows that we will most likely stand against that tactic. However, he may try to con us with lies that may render us immobilized at a pivotal stage of our leadership journey. If you fall into this trap, as I did for years, you may find yourself in a place of fraught idling, and missing out on God's best for your life. Here is how that reality worked against me…

During my early years in ministry, my closest friends were low self-esteem, fear, and insecurity. The enemy knew that tangible cons such as "sex, drugs, and rock-n-roll" would not work against me. By God's grace, I had experienced victory over those pitfalls before they had the opportunity to become part of the fabric of my adult life. However, the enemy had me bound by a life altering CON Game.

For the purpose of this conversation and the context of leadership, allow me to further define what I mean by CON Game. A CON Game is a defeated lifestyle limited by thoughts that confine you to the **Common, Ordinary**, and **Natural**.

This lifestyle is completely devoid of expectancy and the supernatural voice of God. Your eyes are fixed on your limitations and on man. Rather than building God's Kingdom, you are building barriers and excuses around your life.

Too often, those who fall prey to this tactic, resort to imitating those whom they admire. It provides a false narrative and sense of security, progress, and anticipation. You see, many leaders hope that if they behave, speak and think like others, they will eventually also share in their success. Can you see how this can absolutely cripple you and rob you of destiny? Can you also see how there is absolutely no merit in this thought process? It will destroy you from within and over time will atrophy your ministry.

For years, I found myself continually stripped of authority and vision because I made room for the lies of the enemy through the gateway of my mind. Every time a door opened for me, I would freeze. If I did move forward, I would do so in a complete state of fear and doubt.

This cycle ultimately broke me, I could no longer see my way toward a higher purpose. The voice of the Lord was drowned out by the voice of lies. Eventually, my engine stalled and I wasted year after year. This was a painful existence.

I worked hard at justifying this way of life. I tried to make myself feel "okay" about my defeated lifestyle. I knew it was all a lie but I felt powerless against it. I'll never forget the day when I was invited to speak on a panel of New York City ministry leaders. My initial response was a resounding, "Yes!" I was honored and excited to be counted among such dynamic ministry and community leaders. Soon after the invitation, however, I talked myself out of the event, convincing myself that I was not good enough. I sent the host a fabricated reason why I couldn't make it and spent the next few weeks feeling absolutely defeated. This feeling of loss was amplified by the fact that the event was an overwhelming success. So many people were blessed and inspired by it. Sadly, that host never again invited me to one of his leadership forums.

I would like to elaborate on the state of mind in which I existed for most of my young adult years. I believe that the following illustration will paint a good picture for you: Imagine a young skydiver. Before he jumps, he must consider a number of factors.

The average plane filled with skydivers flies at an altitude of approximately 15,000 feet. Once this altitude is reached, the person jumps out of the moving plane. He then begins to fall at a rate of roughly 120 miles per hour. Contrary to how it may appear on TV, this person is not floating gently in the sky like a feather. They are falling fast, like a sack of bricks!

The skydiver has a gauge on his wrist that monitors his altitude and rate of his descent. This is critical because he must pull the chord at 5,000 feet to ensure that he slows down to approximately 10 - 12 miles per hour before touching land. This entire experience takes place in approximately one minute. Yes, 60-seconds! You can only imagine the horrific results if he doesn't follow the directions provided by his instructor.

Now here is the challenge for the person jumping off the plane. For the skydiver who has limited experience, there is an immediate battle between what he knows and what he sees. Upon jumping, their training and knowledge kick in, but so does the emotion and reality that the earth is coming toward the skydiver at 120 miles per hour. So, the person is faced with this hair-raising dilemma. Everything in their mind says, "Pull the chord now – save yourself!" However, if he or she pulls the chord too soon, they may become entangled with the plane or caught by the powerful wind drag created by the plane. This may cause the parachute to deploy incorrectly and ultimately cause immanent death. If the person waits too long, then they may land at a high rate of speed. This high-speed landing may produce a fatal or at minimum a very painful and life altering landing. What to do? Fortunately, most statistics indicate that the majority of skydivers land safely with little or no incident. But the truth, that we are all too aware of, is that there can be things that go wrong and some do experience fatal or severe injuries.

When God calls a leader, as He did Abraham, it can feel very much like a call to jump out of a "plane" into a free fall. There is an immediate battle between what is known as "truth" in Scripture and what one feels in the natural – those emotions often con us into a place of temporary lull or even permanent paralysis. A decision about your ministry or business must be made at this point in your journey. Any indecision now may potentially produce a disastrous crash landing.

As I mentioned earlier, over the years, I battled against this tactic of the enemy. Perhaps you also face this each time the Lord calls you out and reminds you that there is more that He has called you to do. Battles with indecision, intimidation and outright terror about the future can become your thorn in the flesh. If this battle is present in your journey, then you can relate to the Apostle Paul, when he shared both his dilemma, and subsequent declaration of confidence in Christ in 2 Corinthians 12:7-9:

> *"...in order to keep me from becoming conceited, I was given a thorn in my flesh, a messenger of Satan, to torment me. ⁸ Three times I pleaded with the Lord to take it away from me. ⁹ But he said to me, "My grace is sufficient for you, for my power is made perfect in weakness." Therefore, I will boast all the more gladly about my weaknesses, so that Christ's power may rest on me.*

Thankfully, I am no longer a victim of the enemy's ploy. No longer captive. Neither should you remain in that state of limited thinking. Remember, *His grace is sufficient for you.* As you embrace this biblical truth, it will propel you to a place of complete reliance on God's power and sovereignty. When He leads, he is responsible for the victory, not your natural abilities or the lack thereof. We see this idea wholly exemplified in the story of Moses when he began his leadership journey in the second chapter of Exodus.

Moses had been *"educated in all the wisdom of the Egyptians"* and was *"mighty in word and deed."*[1] But his miraculous journey began as a helpless infant in the Nile when Pharaoh's daughter took him away and brought him up as her own son. Clearly, Moses received the best education money and power could offer in that age. The Bible reveals that by the time he was an adult, he was mighty in words and in deeds but Moses himself didn't see it. He complained to God:

> *"Pardon your servant, Lord. I have never been eloquent, neither in the past nor since you have spoken to your servant. I am slow of speech and tongue."*
> **The Lord said to him, "Who gave human beings their mouths? Who makes them deaf or mute? Who gives them sight or makes them blind? Is it not I, the Lord? Now go; I will help you speak and will teach you what to say."**
> *But Moses said, "Pardon your servant, Lord. Please send someone else."*
> *Then the Lord's anger burned against Moses and he said, "What about your brother, Aaron the Levite? I know he can speak well. He is already on his way to meet you, and he will be glad to see you. You shall speak to him and put words in his mouth;* **I will help both of you speak and will teach you what to do.**[2]

Although these were important achievements and perhaps equivalent to a modern-day university degree, this education played no part in the most important stanza of his life. It was not the "wisdom of the Egyptians" that brought about his influence and supernatural impact on the lives of God's people. Simply stated, it was the hand of God. As Scripture says, *"By faith Moses, when he became of age, refused to be called the son of Pharaoh's daughter, choosing rather to suffer affliction with the people of God than to enjoy the passing pleasures of sin, esteeming the reproach of Christ greater riches than the treasures in Egypt; for he looked ahead to his reward."*[3]

I have encountered and survived many con games presented by the enemy. Abraham also faced battles as the Lord brought him to a series of stages where he had to confront some con games that rendered him debilitated. As we read his story, we see how he fell into several of these traps prior to his journey with the Lord. Following are a few of those pitfalls:

1. **Genesis 12: Disobedience** - Abraham was to leave everything and everyone behind, yet he traveled with his father, possessions and others.
2. **Genesis 12 and 13: Fear** - Abraham lied about his wife and said she was his sister, not once but twice.
3. **Genesis 17 and 18: Doubt** - Abraham laughed at the thought that God would provide them with a son.

So how do we carry on with our journey toward continued growth and purpose? The Word calls us to a life that resides above the plane of status quo and the natural so that His Word becomes our fuel. Here are three verses that must become part of our arsenal against the enemy's Con Games:

1. **Isaiah 26:3 NIV:** *"You will keep in perfect peace those whose minds are steadfast, because they **trust** in you."* Trust in God and His word is the launching pad for your leadership journey – go past the limitations that you have placed on yourself. Without trust and faith in Him, you can do nothing.
2. **Romans 12:2 NIV:** *"Do not conform to the pattern of this world, but be **transformed** by the renewing of your mind. Then you will be able to test and approve what God's will is— his good, pleasing and perfect will."* The transformation of your thought life becomes a game changer. The reason why your mind must be transformed is simple. A new mind will no longer contain the old access

points for the enemy to enter or deposit his lies and
manipulations. A renewed mind only has room for
God. Only He has the key. It is fortified,
impenetrable, and filled with His power.

3. **2 Corinthians 10:5 NIV:** *"We **demolish** arguments
   and every pretension that sets itself up against the knowledge of
   God, and we take captive every thought to make it obedient to
   Christ."* Once we decide to trust in the Lord, He
   comes into the picture and brings about a
   transformative work like no man can provide. You are
   then positioned (through the power of Jesus Christ) to
   completely demolish and annihilate all that has been
   set-up against you.

Overcoming Con Games was critical for Abraham; it was
essential to his preparation for the next stage of his journey. We
can name many other great biblical leaders who faced seemingly
insurmountable obstacles with the potential to ground them. Yet,
many believed that God's power would be made perfect in their
weakness[4], and as a result they overcame.

Much hinges on this principle. I call this Abraham's pivot
point. You see, just like a door, Abraham had to position himself
in such a way to allow God's plan to move forward. This is like
the hinges on a door. The hinge determines if a door opens in or
out. Rusted hinges may prevent the door from opening at all.
Likewise, as we make decisions and move throughout our journey, we will experience pivot moments that will determine our
direction, pace and ability to move ahead. Do not remain stuck.
Do not lose out on all that God has for your life. Your freedom is
secure in Him and His Word will always remain true.

REFLECTION

What are the con games from which God has delivered you? How has that positively impact your leadership?

_____
_____
_____
_____
_____
_____
_____
_____
_____
_____

If you are still working through certain con games, take time to identify them. Once you do that, determine how you will overcome. What will you do and whom will you invite into this process?

_____
_____
_____
_____
_____
_____
_____
_____
_____

Can you identify anyone on your team struggling through con games? How can you help them rise above?

_____

_____

_____

_____

_____

_____

_____

_____

_____

_____

_____

_____

_____

_____

_____

_____

_____

_____

_____

_____

_____

_____

_____

1. Acts 7:21-23
2. Exodus 4:10-15 emphasis added
3. Heb 11:24-26
4. 2 Corinthians 12:9

PIT Maneuvers

"When you suffer and lose, that does not mean you are being disobedient to God. In fact, it might mean you're right in the center of His will. The path of obedience is often marked by times of suffering and loss."
— Chuck Swindoll

The way we decode and react to pain throws us into a gear that either drives us forward or reverse. While pain itself is apathetic, it never has an apathetic outcome. Pain will move you at times in ways that may seem arbitrary. However, we all have an innate mode of navigating through pain: "fight, flight, or freeze." Simply stated, it is the way we have handled disagreement, distress, and defeat throughout all our lives, but our standard approach may not be a constructive, or beneficial way to handle discomfort any longer. It is now time for authentic transformation.

Transformation happens when our threshold of longing, or anguish, increases beyond the level of our troubles. Through my leadership journey, I have learned that pain is a breakpoint: it can cause us to wither into a pit and hope it disappears, or it can stimulate new confidence, new strategies, and new desires to learn the lessons it can instill in us.

Do you want to be resilient in this leadership journey you have accepted? If you answered "yes," then you must come to terms with the pain that He allows into your life. Identify it as a catalyst for development and a stage for enhanced efficacy. You will need this perspective in order to move ahead. God has much more in store for you, and it waits beyond your encounter with pain. This viewpoint doesn't diminish the discomfort of the heat we must at times withstand. It simply puts it all in perspective. Yes, the pain is undeniable; there is no rebuffing that. But as we remain open to this experience, another tier of significance is added to our lives: God is employing this process for a grander determination, even if it makes no sense at the time. Do not run from this discomfort. Give it consent to do its work in you.

This reminds me of a story about a woman who had been learning about the refiner's fire in her ladies Bible study. She knew a silversmith and asked him if she could one day drop by his shop to watch him work. She didn't tell him her purpose in being there but just watched quietly as he went about refining the silver in his shop. She was surprised to note that his face was so close to the furnace and he seemed to be watching intently as the silver with impurities melted and was refined. His face was red and beaded with sweat.

She asked him, "Can't you back up? It's terribly hot." He shook his head, "I need to watch carefully until the impurities are burned away. Once they are, I need to remove the silver quickly." "How do you know when the impurities are gone?" the woman asked. "When I can see my reflection in it." The silversmith responded.

Isn't that a perfect description? God allows us at times to enter the fire allowing it to burn away our impurities but no matter how it feels, He is never far away. He is close to us, watching carefully until He sees his reflection clearly in us. Then, and only then, He move us out of the fire.

This lesson became a reality to me in 2001, when my boss informed me that the company had been sold and that our entire department would be disbanded as a result of this transaction. No details were provided; we were left in the dark. Every day I would call my boss to see if we were still employed. I could not believe this was happening to me. My wife was expecting our second child and soon I would be unemployed. I had no idea that the plot would soon thicken, and my life would be tossed into even greater turmoil and chaos.

As this drama developed, my wife was entering her eighth month of pregnancy. Soon after, she realized that something was terribly wrong. Her belly continued to grow at an unusual pace, and she began to feel tremendously ill. Her doctor minimized the symptoms at first until her scheduled ultrasound proved that there was something awry. There was an excess of amniotic fluid and it became very difficult to see the baby. The doctor immediately referred us to the chief obstetrician at the hospital.

I will never forget the feeling of despair as we sat in that waiting room to meet the new doctor - just moments after learning about the complication with our pregnancy. Special tests had been performed in advance of this appointment and we were anxious to hear the news. All we knew at this juncture was that the baby was alive. Finally, we were called in to meet the doctor. He was kind and gentle, clearly knowledgeable and prepared to deal with this "high risk" pregnancy. Yet this did not lessen the weight of what might be ahead of us.

The doctor took time to review the results and images from the ultrasound, and blood work. In short, he said, the excess amniotic fluid is an indication of a chronic abnormality with the child. The child may be born severely deformed, down syndrome, or have any combination of serious medical issues. The list was too long to discuss at length. He asked that we return to the waiting room while he consulted with his team and then he would call us back in to discuss a game plan.

It felt like the longest walk in my life, as I walked out of the doctor's office to an empty seat in the waiting room. In that moment, all I could hear was my accelerated heartbeat and the breath entering and exiting my lungs. The sterilized scent of that pristine office heightened my awareness that our next steps would most likely lead us to an emergency room. I was gripped by panic, and uncertainty. A windstorm of questions began to swirl in my mind.

Once I returned to my seat, the wait seemed eternal. My wife and I sat there in complete silence. We must have appeared cata-tonic – no emotion or movement! However, I was in deep and desperate dialogue with the Lord. I kept asking Him, "Why, Lord? How could this be?" "There has to be a mistake here!" I continued this desperate pleading with the Lord until I was mentally exhausted. Finally, my mind quieted and I made room for Him to respond.

It was as if I heard Him whisper a life changing response into my ear. He simply said, "This is the road before you. You only have two choices. You can proceed with Me, or you can proceed alone." Tears began to well up in my eyes and I responded, "With you, Lord! I will proceed with you."

That was one of my toughest "pit" moments. It was dark and hopeless, until I invited Jesus on the journey. Don't get me wrong! It was an arduous experience and we had to endure much, espe-cially my wife. I eventually shared with my wife the conversation I had with the Lord as we waited for the doctor, and she agreed that we had to trust the Lord. Abortion was not an option. We would have this baby and love him no matter the outcome.

After several grueling days in the hospital, our miracle boy was born. He was beautiful. But our journey did not end there. His deformity was not external. It was internal. The following morning, he was rushed into emergency surgery to reconstruct his small intestine in order to remove a blockage that would unquestionably claim his young life.

This was the issue we had been preparing to face and when it was finally upon us, God wonderfully superintended this process. We were assigned to a world-renowned pediatric surgeon. He was about to enter retirement, but he agreed to stay on and perform the delicate and complicated surgery. We had several hours of waiting before we were given an update. The surgeon came to speak to us directly, and our breaths caught in the seconds before he said, "The surgery was a success."

My wife and I let out a deep sigh of relief, but again, the journey was not over. Meeting our eyes the surgeon continued to say, "Your son is very frail, premature and the best-case scenario of his survival is 50/50."

He did his best to encourage us, but that dark pit was still our place of residence. Our son was moved to the neonatal intensive care unit where he remained for approximately one month. We saw him improve some days and we also faced setbacks with serious complications. Several times a day, during this season, we visited our son, held his 3-pound body in our hands and sang to him, prayed over him and read Scriptures to him. We chose to walk through this pit with Jesus. It wasn't easy, but we did it.

So how did this story end? Well, my employer said that we would remain on salary, but were not allowed to do any work. We simply had to check in with him until the sale was finalized. That allowed me the flexibility to be at the hospital multiple times a day for the entire month that my son was in the intensive care unit. It also allowed me to be there for my wife as she navigated this reality.

As for my son, he was eventually strong enough to come home and continue his long journey of recovery. Today, he is healthy, tall, strong, and a college student. He plays piano and guitar and loves to sing to the Lord as he serves on the worship team at our church. And it brings such joy to my heart to report that his burning passion is to one day serve the Lord full-time as a worship minister. I have no doubt that he will achieve his dream.

Only God could have written this story. But I often ask myself, what might have happened if I had pushed God away and lifted a fist to heaven rather than an open heart? I am so thankful that when it mattered most, my foundational faith in God compelled me to choose Him while in the pit.

That is my story, but I know this is how God often causes us to grow in our understanding of who He is. It is also how God causes us to grow in our understanding of who we are and the many things that we must surrender to Him. If the realities of leadership life at times drag us into a scary and dark pit, I think that we should then spend time exploring the concept of 'Pit Maneuvers.' We'll do this by taking a bird's eye look at Joseph's story in the book of Genesis.

> *A few days later Israel (Jacob) called for Joseph, and told him, "Your brothers are over in Shechem grazing the flocks. Go and see how they are getting along, and how it is with the flocks, and bring me word." "Very good," Joseph replied. So he traveled to Shechem from his home at Hebron Valley. A man noticed him wandering in the fields…*[1]

> Genesis 37:13-14

We continue to read in Genesis 37:23-24:

> *So when Joseph got there, they (his brothers) pulled off his brightly colored robe, and threw him into an empty well —there was no water in it.*

Joseph is eventually sold to Potiphar, here we see that he experienced some success, even though he was a slave.[2] Potiphar's wife destroys Joseph's gig with a horrible lie. He winds up in Jail for a crime he did not commit.[3]

At this leg of his journey, we learn something powerful about God's involvement in Joseph's story. In this thirty-ninth chapter of Genesis, we read three times, "The Lord was with Joseph." This serves as a reminder to us that even though Joseph was in a dire situation, God was always with him. No matter how dark the circumstances, God remained actively engaged in Joseph's life. This should serve as an encouragement to us. We should never judge God's involvement or level of activity in our journey by the good or bad times we experience. I can attest to that in my life!

He is the constant factor in the life of a healthy leader. He is the barometer who sets the tone. He is not subject to other variables or happenings. He is the one who determines all things in our lives. So, as you go through your life, know that if you are honoring God and living for him and his people, He will continue to lead you. He will continue to influence and move things so that you reach your destination. He's got your back.

Further in his story, we see that Joseph ascends to be number two in all of Egypt. The story is well known... Yet it still amazes us because it is a reminder of all God can do in and through us when we outright yield to Him.

In Genesis 50:20[4], we see Joseph speak some of the most powerful words in the Bible,

> *"As far as I am concerned, God turned into good what you meant for evil, for he brought me to this high position I have today so that I could save the lives of many people."*

So, what was the purpose of Joseph's PIT? We just read the answer in Genesis 50:20. Joseph's pit was used to bring about the saving of God's people during a massive famine in the land. It also set the stage for the future liberation of God's people through His servant Moses.

Now I must ask you, "What is the purpose of the pit you are now in or soon to be in?" Have you given any thought to that question? Most people will often fail to consider the "what" behind their pit experience. They do so because they are stuck on the "why." When you ask "why," you are often in a state of pity and complaint. "Why me God? Why me?"

However, when you ask "what," you are asking for revelation. You are asking God to show you what He is doing. When you ask God a "what" question, you are asking Him to reveal His heart and plan to you. Here is the great part of this truth: As God responds to your "what" questions, He also reveals why! He is so awesome. So, let's take a moment to break this down a bit and explore two broad purposes behind the pit experience:

1. Ultimately, a pit experience is introduced into our lives to give God glory. (2 Corinthians 4:17 NIV) "For our light and momentary affliction is producing for us an eternal glory that is far beyond comparison."

2. A pit experience will often be used by God to refine us into the person who is best equipped to bring about that glory to Him. God allowed Joseph to be broken and humbled before raising him up into leadership. We can glean from the story that Joseph had a leadership gifting, but he also had a lot of pride. However, he seemed unaware of its effect on his life and family. That pride would have gotten in the way of his service to God and he would not have been a renowned biblical leader. He needed to be humbled. The methods of his humiliation allowed, and possibly prepared, by God seem to be too extreme and to last far too long, but only God knows the state of our

heart. He is the refiner who is looking for his reflection in the silver, and He alone knows when He sees it.

With that in mind, I want to share three principles that will help you better understand the PIT experience and how it can bring glory to God and refine you as well. Since we often ask questions during times of testing, let's take that route for the next few moments. Following are several ideas and questions that should help you examine your heart the next time you find yourself in a pit that is testing your peace and causing you to question the one you are following:

P.I.T. Maneuvers

Perpetually Learn: *What knowledge am I gaining today that I didn't have access to yesterday?*

This was the beginning of Joseph's transformation as he began his journey in that dark and cold pit. He had to embrace new habits, ideas and concepts. When we become open receptacles, we are then positioned to receive from God, mentors, books, and those who are leading around us in excellence. Proverbs 1:5 says,

> *"Let the wise hear and increase in learning, and the one who understands obtain guidance."*

When I found myself in the pit, facing the challenges of my son's complicated birth, I had to learn to be still and listen to His leading. I had to learn to accept His comfort. I also had to learn to surrender my understanding to His sovereignty.

Intentionally Unlearn: *What did I release today that I believed yesterday?*

We don't see Joseph making the same error over and over

again. There was grounding and maturing that took place in his life. We must experience the same as we endure tough moments in our leadership life. To walk in this new paradigm, leaders must allow new understanding and knowledge to push out old ways that will no longer move them forward and upward.

Too many people are taught important lessons but hold onto their old ways. The old mindsets cancel out the effect of the new ideas. There is only room for one paradigm and the new one should take precedence. This takes time and intentionality. Joseph was in the "pit" for approximately sixteen years. There was a prolonged and emotional process in this man's life. Most people are more comfortable with old problems than with new solutions. Don't allow that to become your reality. That will keep you paralyzed and will halt your growth and development. This concept is presented to us in Ephesians 4:22-24, where we read,

"put off your old self, which belongs to your former manner of life and is corrupt through deceitful desires, and to be renewed in the spirit of your minds, and to put on the new self, created after the likeness of God in true righteousness and holiness."

During my pit season, I had to unlearn the old habit of defeated thinking. That modality had been my go-to mindset and it would no longer work for me in this new arena of faith. The Bible reminds us to continually surrender ourselves to the Lord.[5]

Tenaciously Relearn: *What am I changing today that I did yesterday?*

Joseph was able to continue learning and repackaging himself over the years so as to meet the ever changing call on his life during each unique season. We saw this in the pit, Potiphar's house and even in the palace. We also saw this when he encountered his family after years of separation. He had choices to make, emotions to confront and scars to heal. His approach from earlier years could no longer carry him where he stood at that moment.

Moreover, the strategies of the moment would most likely not suffice for tomorrow's challenge. Joseph's flexibility and teachability granted him amazing success. This paradigm is the very thing that will set the stage for your next great leadership feat.

Likewise, the experience of my son's birth brought along many lessons, but I did not stop learning when that experience was over. I have given myself room to continue to learn and to course correct as often as necessary. Anything short of that is simply unacceptable if I am to lead my family and those whom I serve in ministry and in business.

Here is a truth to consider: If what you learned 10 years ago still excites you today, you may be in a heap of trouble. You must remain open to new idea, and continue to learn and grow. Yesterday's knowledge should not fully satisfy your thirst today. You should not exclusively look to your past to make it through today. Remembering God's provision in the past is not necessarily a bad thing, but it should no longer be your singular basis of sustenance. Build on the past, but don't live there.

John Maxwell once shared a story about a gentleman who approached him after a seminar. The man shook John's hand and said, "I wish I would have heard you teach today's lesson ten years ago. It would have transformed my life, and I would have avoided so many mistakes along the way." John smiled and responded, "That would have been impossible my friend. You see, ten years ago, I didn't know what I taught you today. I've grown over the last ten years, and so I am now able to teach you as I did today." The highs and lows of life formed John's perspective and knowledge in his walk and in the leadership arena. That in turn positioned him to share this information with others and stir them onto good works and greater exploits.

Let's review what we've covered in the last few pages: Perpetually Learn, Intentionally Unlearn, and Tenaciously Relearn. As you observed in Joseph's story, and even in my story, this is often easier said than done. Nonetheless, it is doable, and it is the key to forward movement in your leadership passage. So, keep this one thing in mind, God is with you and He is often leading you to and through a PIT season.

As such, some of your toughest battles in life will be with God. Why? The default, sinful, nature in each of us is set to resist the will of God and it has to be dealt with intentionally and continually. Until you're willing to undergo an honest assessment and then respond truthfully, your life will never change for the better. Your impact will be limited, and you will not experience the full weight of your purpose. With that in mind, I must ask you, "Do you really want the blessing of God over your life?" Before you answer that question, first stop and ask yourself these questions:

1. Am I willing to let go of what I want if it's not God's will for me?
2. Do I covet what others have instead of waiting for God's unique provision for me?
3. Do I keep talking about my rights because I haven't fully surrendered to the Lord?
4. Do I truly love others and think of them first?
5. Am I practicing the daily disciplines of prayer and Bible reading?
6. Am I trusting God to reproduce the character of Jesus in me so that I might be able to express joy in the midst of adversity?

Not only will your answers to these questions determine your discipleship temperament and destiny, but they will also determine your level of blessing and your level of impact in the lives of those whom you serve. Take a moment to meditate on the words found in Hebrews 10:35-36,

"So do not throw away your confidence; it will be richly rewarded. You need to persevere so that when you have done the will of God, you will receive what he has promised."

REFLECTION

What are some practical ways to "relearn" or continue to grow after a "pit" season?

_____

_____

_____

_____

_____

_____

_____

_____

_____

_____

What are the skills and perspectives that you will require to lead people out of a sustained season of difficulty?

_____

_____

_____

_____

_____

_____

_____

_____

_____

_____

_____

_____

How do you currently lead in difficult times? Is there anything that you should surrender to the Lord and replace with His approach?

_____

_____

_____

_____

_____

_____

_____

_____

_____

_____

_____

_____

_____

_____

_____

_____

_____

_____

_____

_____

_____

_____

---

1. Living Bible (TLB)
2. Genesis 39:1-2
3. Genesis 39:12-23
4. Living Bible (TLB)
5. 1 Chronicles 16:11

4

"D" is For Destiny

"Nothing splendid has ever been achieved except by those who dared believe that something inside them was superior to circumstance."
— *Bruce Barton*

In Exodus 2:11-15 we read about the early stage of Moses' leadership journey. It is a story filled with scenarios that can rival Hollywood's greatest movies. Actually, some would say that *The Ten Commandments* was one of Hollywood's greatest movies; but you know what I mean. The story in Exodus is filled with fascinating details about one man's impact on the people he led – the people he loved. It is replete with incredible miracles and feats that most of us can only dream about. However, it is more than anything, a story about one man's battle against his insecurities and the call on his life. In the man, Moses, we see fear, disobedience, insecurities, failure and so much more. That same list can be built for most of us!

The thing that makes this story so miraculous is that in the midst of all that human frailty, we see how God is faithful to the call on His servant's life. We also see God's faithfulness to His promises both to one man and one nation. There is much about this story to which I can not relate because of the sheer size of the call placed on Moses' life. However, there is much more about this story to which I can relate and see in my own humanity.

The journey taken by Moses is one filled with mystery, pain, great joy, excitement and lest we forget – astonishing miracles. There are segments of his journey that, if we had our druthers, we would love, and then there are those we would altogether avoid. In this story, we see how a man who is on his way to become a powerful leader in Egypt is suddenly hit with an unexpected detour and a series of events that would forever change his life and the world around him.

When we arrive at the second chapter of Exodus, we find a Moses already aware of the fact that Hebrew blood ran through his veins. For some reason, the Bible doesn't share details about his childhood in Egypt, and experience as a Hebrew teen living the life of Egyptian royalty.

At this point in the story, we see a man in search of his identity. A man in search of a story that would help him pull all the pieces of the puzzle together. We see a man in pursuit of his purpose in the midst of a convoluted existence.

Have you ever felt like that? Have you ever wondered where those missing parts of your puzzle reside? So many of us begin our search for those missing pieces at a young age, and we find ourselves whispering private questions to the Lord. "Why am I this way? What caused me to be fearful about life? Who am I, Lord? Who am I... really?"

This process we see Moses go through, is remarkably similar

to the process God chooses to use in our lives as leaders today. Why? It is a process that ensures that His predetermined purpose for your life comes to fruition. While this progression primarily changes and impacts our inner persona, it also has much to do with the people we will ultimately serve and influence for God's kingdom. You see, the purpose of this experience of self-discovery and metamorphosis is to bring us to a place where we become moldable, usable and effective as His vessels.

If we go back to take another look at Moses and his situation, we can say that he was in a prime position and location for maximum influence over God's people and the government that held them captive. He was in essence a young leader who had the ear of the ruling family.

Why not use Moses where he was? That is a fair question on the surface, but we have to look deep into the person of Moses and deep into the heart of God to fully understand. First of all, let us be clear that it was God who set His people free from captivity. It could not have been Pharaoh or his government. It could not have been Moses' effort as a government official, or any man for that matter. It had to be God through His servant, as this was the only way that He would have received all glory and honor from His people. It was also the only way for other nations to see that the God of the Hebrew nation was in fact an all-powerful and proximate God.

There was also a great work that had to take place in Moses. Much of what resided in his heart and mind had to be purged. This typically takes place through experiences that are often painful and difficult. I would liken it to the removal of a splinter from one's finger. Sometimes, it is a protracted and painful process, especially if the splinter has worked its way deep under the skin. However, once the splinter, or foreign object is removed, there is almost immediate relief, and normal use of that finger is gained once again.

God had to remove unhealthy and foreign 'splinters' from

Moses' heart and mind so that he could then be filled with God's mind and God's ways. In this manner, Moses became an extension of God's hand and a deliverer of God's words both to His people and to their captor.

While there are many ways to explain and illustrate how God brings us through this transformative process, I would like to capture this journey by detailing three essential stages. This is what I call the road to destiny. While on this road, we are forced to confront a myriad of realities that have gone unnoticed or avoided at times for years. But as you embrace the work of the Lord in your life, you will immediately begin to see His rationale and His heart, which ultimately reveals His purpose.

Exciting, isn't it? Think about it. The God of all creation decides to break through eternity, reach down and touch the life of a sinner— saved by grace— like you or me. He does all this with an eye toward an invitation into a journey of a lifetime. Can it get any better than that? Absolutely not!

I want you to move past the fear, the uncertainties and the pain often associated with this road. Now let's focus on the fact that an almighty, all-knowing, and never-changing God loves you enough to consider you a part of His master plan for humanity. Take a moment right now and think about that truth. Write down some thoughts about that reality and consider the grandeur of the plan that has you in the center of all the excitement.

I struggled with this idea for years. Why would God wish to use a flawed man like me to have any impact on humanity? Why would He use a man, as simple as I am, to inspire or challenge leaders? The answer is clear. It is His prerogative. He uses whom He wishes. Only He knows the "why" behind His choices. You and I simply must rejoice and accept the honor of being hand selected by the King of the entire universe.

Now, let's take a look at this process with a new perspective and sense of anticipation of what God wishes to say to us and do in us by way of His plan.

Divine Dissociation

Webster's Dictionary defines Dissociation as: *to end your relationship with or connection to someone or something; to separate (yourself) from someone or something.*

As God leads you down this route, He will remove you from relationships and environments that may be sinful, unproductive, or simply a distraction from your destination. You may not see these things or people as I just described, but if He says they are, then who are we to argue with the God of Heaven?

In Moses' case, God removed him as an infant from an obscure village and placed him in the opulence, power and grandeur of the Egyptian royal family. For forty years, he enjoyed these indulgences. As we touched on in earlier chapters he also enjoyed the very best training and education the world could offer any man. Most Egyptian leaders spoke several languages and were skilled as engineers, scholars and much more. This was the backdrop of Moses' daily life. But while Moses was still physically in this environment, his heart began to draw closer to the Hebrew people - his people. This was not Moses' doing, but rather the very hand of God changing him a bit at a time.

As this transformation took place, he began to feel compassion toward the Hebrew captives and their dreadful work conditions. He took notice of the abuse and eventually acted in haste and with no consideration of repercussions. Unfortunately, one day, he killed an Egyptian in retaliation to the abuse that was being perpetrated on a Hebrew slave. When watching the movie adaptation, at this point in the story you hear dramatic music as the backdrop to this riveting scene! Perhaps Moses, at this juncture, thought that his influence would pave the way to freedom. Perhaps in his mind, he thought that God would use his sincere actions to free His people. Though he was sincere, he was sincerely wrong!

In his heart, Moses believed he did the right thing. But that was the core of Moses' greatest challenge. He did what was right in his eyes, without the leading of God as well as His timing. Now he had to face the consequences of his actions. He would spend the next forty years in the desert coming to grip with this reality. The act of murder by one Egyptian against another was punishable by death. So, Moses had no choice but to flee into the desert. He had to abandon everything he had and everything he knew and in return, he received the anguish of isolation. It must have felt like an eternity. Can you imagine Moses reaching the desert, leaning against a boulder and crying out to the heavens, "I don't deserve this punishment! I meant to do what was right! Why me?"

This is usually a painful process that can potentially create significant wounds and need for subsequent healing. Many leaders find themselves in a similar place early in their journey. Some may even find themselves in this place multiple times throughout their journey.

God will often lift you up and out of current circumstances and environments to eradicate anything that will hinder, delay or even halt His plan for your life. I've been there. I can remember how God removed my wife and I from relationships and places that were not in line with His forward plan. They had their purpose and season, but it was now time to move on. As mentioned earlier, this often causes great pain and at times even resentment and many questions.

When you are disassociated and adrift there seems to be a deafening silence that can appear to consume you but it is in this place that we begin to hear the voice of God. This is where God quiets all noises and all other voices. This is where His voice becomes familiar and clearer.

As leaders, one of the first areas of development must be our ability to hear the voice of God. God desires such intimacy with us that we would instantly recognize His voice in a sea of competing voices and distractions. To achieve that, He will often remove familiar voices. He will remove familiar resources and yes, even crutches that we learn to lean on during times of ambiguity. He wants us to learn the sound and cadence of His voice. This is not an instant process or an overnight experience, but it is a life altering experience, nonetheless.

Over the years, and on multiple occasions, I have found myself disassociated and desperately searching for a voice that would provide direction or answers. Through anxious prayers and pleading I have learned to trust, and each day that goes by, I find myself closer to Him and more familiar with that sweet still voice.

In Exodus 3:1-6, we see that Moses is introduced to the clear voice of God. There was no noise or distraction. He had long been removed from the royal palace and protocols. There were no more royal niceties, or conflicting demands that could distract or interfere. It was Moses and God. This is where he became familiar with the voice of his God. It reads as follows:

> *Now Moses was tending the flock of Jethro his father-in-law, the priest of Midian, and he led the flock to the far side of the wilderness and came to Horeb, the mountain of God. There the angel of the Lord appeared to him in flames of fire from within a bush. Moses saw that though the bush was on fire it did not burn up. So Moses thought, "I will go over and see this strange sight—why the bush does not burn up."*
> *When the Lord saw that he had gone over to look, God called to him from within the bush, "Moses! Moses!"*
> *And Moses said, "Here I am."*
> *"Do not come any closer," God said. "Take off your sandals, for the place where you are standing is holy ground." Then he said, "I am the God of your father, the God of Abraham, the God of Isaac and the God of*

Jacob." At this, Moses hid his face, because he was
afraid to look at God. (NIV)

In this portion of Scripture, we see God breakthrough a long
season of silence. He came before His servant in a spectacular
way. This encounter forever changed the man who was plucked
out of an obscure village, placed in the home of the Egyptian
ruler, and then escaped into a dry and desolate place. This
journey could have annihilated the best of us. That is why I
believe God took the time to present Himself in such a powerful
and personal manner. He knew that Moses, His servant, needed
a supernatural jumping point. Moses needed a game-changing
event.

In this exchange, God accomplished many things. He got
Moses' attention. For some of us we may see this happen in the
loss of a job or a painful transition in ministry. Either way, God
knows how to get our attention.

He then said to Moses, *"I am the God of your father, the God of*
Abraham, the God of Isaac and the God of Jacob." It is as if, God
seared into Moses' heart the realization that he stood before the
One spoken of and worshipped by those who came before him.
God put things in context for Moses. Moses reacted by hiding his
face at the realization of his present company. It was a powerful
moment as the God of the Hebrew people revealed himself to a
runaway Hebrew-Egyptian royal turned future leader of Israel.

This is an understanding that we must all obtain in our leadership journey. I had my own experience of coming face-to-face
with my frail humanity and great need of an all-powerful God
when I was just twenty years old. The Lord revealed Himself to
me when I found myself in the deepest and driest moment of
my life: my dear grandfather – my friend, hero and constant
role model had died. His passing rocked my world, and for a
time I turned my back on everything and everyone. I said good-
bye to relationships, church, ministry and yes, even to God.

After all, in my mind, He was the one who took my dear grand-father away!

For six months, I journeyed and experimented with the "plea-sures" of the world. Thankfully, I had my burning bush moment where God clearly called me back home. That was an unplanned visit to my old home church with my drinking buddy. I sat in that sanctuary and listened to a genuine Gospel message for the very first time. Everything in me shook. I heard the voice of God calling me back into relationship with Him. His voice was clear, and just like Moses, I felt compelled to draw near to that flame. As I did, I removed my proverbial sandals and surrendered to Jesus, the Son of God. My life would never be the same.

As with Moses, this experience set the ground for the next stage of my leadership journey. In the midst of grief, I learned the most about God and even about myself. Aspects of faith that had once been only knowledge became my personal experience. I now had an intimate understanding of His grace and sovereignty. I realized that He never lost track of me, or the plan that He had for me. Nothing was wasted. He superintended my detour and brought me right back to where I belonged. These moments help us to face the reality of who we truly are and what resides in us. In this place, we are positioned to surrender all at His feet.

Moments like these should not be wasted on evaluation of people who hurt us or failed us during this process. We must simply comply, surrender and experience His amazing work in our lives. As we do this, He will reveal and heal, as he deems necessary.

Now, I would fail you if I weren't candid about the years of my surrender and renewal. Those transformative experiences came with their share of temptations and challenges. The truth is that before I completely surrendered, I found myself focusing on how a particular pastor hurt me, or a brother failed me. In hind-sight, I can tell you that this mindset delayed the work that God was endeavoring to bring about in my life. Thankfully, my journey did not end in defeat. As time passed I was able to release all that was weighing me down and turned my eyes back to Jesus.

In short, we will encounter the "woe is me" syndrome in this stage of God's work in us; but must not settle there. Allow God to move you onto your next phase of this transformative progression.

Once Moses embraced where he was and before whom he stood, he was positioned to receive purpose, encouragement and guidance from God. We see this in Exodus 3:10-12:

> So now, go. I am sending you to Pharaoh to bring my people the Israelites out of Egypt." [11] But Moses said to God, "Who am I that I should go to Pharaoh and bring the Israelites out of Egypt?" And God said, "I will be with you. And this will be the sign to you that it is I who have sent you: When you have brought the people out of Egypt, you will worship God on this mountain."

The Lord gave Moses clear instructions about his mission. Now this was no insignificant task. Moses was instructed to go before the Pharaoh – the most powerful man in their world, and tell him that he was to free the Hebrews.

Moses was quick to give God excuses and reasons why he was not equipped for this job. Likewise, this is the time when we instinctively fight God. We go into survival mode. We resist Him. We question Him and explain to Him why He is so wrong in choosing us. However, if we move past that turmoil, we can begin our forward march in Him. You notice that I said, "*if* we move past..." In other words, this emotion and struggle is legitimate. No one expects you to not feel these things. However, you are not to reside there, as this could become the demise of your spiritual leadership.

As with Moses, this is when we can experience a greater understanding of who God is and what he desires to do in and through our lives. This is where we develop "Stand Alone Faith." Here is the place where our dependence is solely on God and not man. Every leader needs a faith that stands on the merit and promises of God. Do you have "stand alone faith?"

If you answered "no," then this is an ideal time to ask for that in your life. Tell Him what you need. Let Him know that you desire to forge ahead with Him. Invite Him deeper into your leadership journey. You will begin to experience a fortification in your spirit like never before. The journey does not become easier. However, you will find that it takes much more to bring you to a breaking point. You will not quickly raise the white flag and surrender to the enemy. In due time, you will begin to build resistance. You will begin to see beyond the battle and envision your victory. Divine dissociation positions you for the greatest journey of your life. You will drop what weighs you down and will take on the one Who gives flight to your purpose. Now that is not a bad deal!

Divine Discovery

As we saw earlier, God had Moses move out of his little village in his infancy and brought him to the Pharaoh's palace – a seat of power and prominence. While in Egypt, for forty years, Moses functioned as a mover and shaker - even as the Lord revealed to him that he was a Hebrew. This allowed Moses to interact and learn from some of Egypt's greatest minds and most powerful and influential leaders. This did not go to waste in the desert and the years that followed! This would become a significant play in his mandate from heaven – *"Let My People go…"*

While you are experiencing the Divine Discovery phase of your journey, you are to continue to serve, grow and learn. Strive to better understand yourself and serve where you are – even if it hurts! This will be the very arsenal that God uses to elevate you in His kingdom. This is your time to learn as much as you can so that you become effective in His Kingdom.

Where has God called you? How big a dream has He given you? This is the stage where you and He begin to discuss these very things. This is where you receive clarity on your purpose – scope, size, time, etc. It is through this process that I discovered my purpose.

One day, I sat in the office of a pastor and mentor, sharing with him my burning desire to discover and understand my divine purpose and role in the Kingdom of God. So, we began a discussion that would mark me for the rest of my life.

This Pastor pulled out a white board and wrote the word purpose. He then instructed me to sit silently and ask God to reveal to me the purpose of my life. Quite honestly, I was a bit bewildered and looked at him with a bemused grin on my face. He again said, "John, close your eyes and ask God to speak to you. Ask Him to reveal your purpose."

So, I sat there and began to quietly pray. As I did, I heard myself talking to God and repeating to Him the many titles that I have heard people speak into my life. One of those was the role of "pastor." I struggled to share that one with my mentor because I felt unworthy and unqualified, just as Moses did when God called him to lead. I eventually mustered the courage to look up at this pastor and I muttered the word "Pastor?"

He smiled, and said, "I don't disagree with you John, but that may be the vehicle the God uses to reveal or use your purpose. However, that is not your purpose." Now I was really confused. He saw how befuddled I looked and elaborated his point, "Continue to ask the Lord and believe that He will speak to you." I started to understand what he was getting at and began to pray with a different mindset.

I no longer asked God to reveal my title or function in a church or ministry. I endeavored to discover my purpose in Him and that is when He spoke to me. I suddenly began to cry. I heard the word, but initially it did not make sense to me. You see, we often don't immediately understand God's messages because our minds are so finite. That is why we must not be too quick to run, after speaking with the Lord. We must linger and hear His heart. As I did just that, the one word that resonated in my heart, the only word I could hear and see in my mind's eyes was: BUILDER.

At that moment, I understood that God had called me to be a builder and it was clear to me what it meant. The Pastor did not have to explain it to me; I knew what it meant because God Himself spoke the word into my heart. I knew that I was to be a builder of people who God wanted to use as leaders in His kingdom. I also understood that I was to be a builder of healthy organizations – for His glory. I realized that, in previous years, I had developed skills and passions that I thought were simply geared toward a career or salary. However, God had taken ownership of those skills for His purpose in my life.

All this transpired in just minutes. I then looked up at my mentor with tears running down my face and he smiled and said, "He told you!" I nodded and said, "yes." I then proceeded to share my experience and my personal mission statement. To this day, I repeat it as often as I can because it is real to me. It is an expression of who I am and what God has done in me through this process of discovery.

Over the years, I have studied and gleaned from great academic leaders and powerful ministry and business leaders. As a result, information and experiences gleaned from these unique encounters have continued to shape me into the servant leader that I am today.

Now I understand that the calling from heaven requires strong leaders and ministries that can bear the weight. I have the pleasure of being His hands extended to others so that they too may experience all He has for them. God has graciously equipped me with understanding and grace to communicate strategies and truths that can become foundational to the vision of churches and leaders. But this came as a result of embracing **Dissociation and Discovery** in my pursuit of God's purpose for my life. This came as a result of loss and betrayal. This came as a result of deafening silence during long periods of time, when all I wanted was a comforting word from my Lord. This came as a result of tears and determination not to surrender to the voice that often beckoned me to quit and walk away.

I urge you to use this time wisely and see all that God has to show you and has to tell you. This is not wasted time; this is not time lost. If it wasn't wasted time for Moses during his 40 years of nomad existence in the desert, neither will it be for you. Find godly people in whom you can confide. Share with them and tell them about your journey. Invite them into a covenant of prayer and accountability. This will position you on a high ground of integrity and strength that will carry you further than you can ever imagine. How? As you enter this place of consecration, you are now inviting the Holy Spirit into a place of intimate sojourning. He is now free to speak, to challenge and inspire you into a deeper place of understanding and acceptance of your purpose as a servant leader and most importantly as a child of the living God. These choices and steps ultimately lead to the third and final stage toward your Destiny.

Divine Discontent

I am sure you have heard of or read about the term, "divine discontent." Here is some food for thought: Have you ever found yourself walking and all of a sudden you feel a sharp pain on the sole of your foot? You try to ignore it, but you can't. You realize that it is caused by a small pebble or object in your shoe that is the culprit and cause of your discomfort. You then begin to shake your foot as you walk. You try to do this inconspicuously so as to avoid unwanted attention from those around you. Eventually, you arrive at the conclusion that you must stop and address the issue. Even then, you try to shift and shake the item to the front of your shoe thinking that there will be a void where the small object will remain and not affect you any longer. You take another few steps and realize that your hypothesis was flawed.

At this juncture, you acquiesce to the reality of your situation, remove your shoe, shake the small torture devise out of your shoe and proceed onto your destination. Now, as you take your first pain free steps, you realize that you should have removed the item from your shoe long before this moment. Nonetheless, you are now unfettered from the former pain and distraction, and you are free to move on.

As you embrace the work of God in your life, you will notice that there will be things around you that will invigorate you. Conversely, you will also find that there are things that make you feel outraged and troubled. Divine Discontent is that uncomfortable feeling that often comes from heaven and compels you to act in a clear and decisive manner. It is that proverbial small pebble in your shoe that moves us out of complacency! Yes, that's why it's there. If you had the problems of the pebble without the pain, it may eventually cause injury and even small injuries can lead to infection. So God gives us the gift of pain to point out problems. Still we will often try to ignore it, at least until there is a convenient or less disconcerting time to deal with it, but eventually we will have no choice but to come to grips with the matter at hand. This is usually a significant indicator of the depth of what God desires to do in our lives. The thing that God desires to do is in direct proportion to our purpose and function in this life and His Kingdom.

As for me, that pebble manifests whenever I see deficient leadership behaviors, innocuous vision and waning passion for evangelism and discipleship. Yes, that gets me going, especially, as it relates to the local church. You ask why? Simple. When I see the above workings, I know that the net result will be fewer lives transformed by the Gospel and fewer Christians experiencing their purpose in the body of Christ. These realities bring about eternal dividends that will absolutely payout, whether for good or for evil. Now some of you may think that I am being a bit dramatic by using the word "evil" in this context. Let's take a moment to see what the Word of God has to say:

> *"Remember, it is sin to know what you ought to do and then not do it."*

> James 4:17

We should not remain in that state of apathy, nor should we allow others in our circles to remain either. Before I arrived to a place where I could articulate this idea, I had to endure many "pebbles" in my shoes. Over the course of many years of ministry and business endeavors, the Lord has used the pain and challenges of life to help me understand His wonderful design deep inside my heart. I am a byproduct of the journey that I have experienced over many years. There is no coincidence here. God's masterful plan brought me through the ideal training that compels me today to serve at the level and capacity that I do – and I love every minute of it.

Now back to our friend Moses. After he left Egypt, Moses found himself in the desert for 40 years. During that time, God did a transformative work in his life. Moses was now positioned to learn about the pebbles in his sandals! He was able to dialogue with himself and more importantly with God. His passion for God's people became clear and genuine to him. This was necessary so that at the opportune moment, he would be able to understand his purpose and be willing to face the giant called Pharaoh with a message from God. This was not wasted time for Moses and it will not be wasted time for you, my friend.

Complete Dependence

Moses returned to Egypt as a tested and transformed leader (even though he still did not perceive himself as such). He had a better understanding of what stirred his heart as well as the heart of God. He could no longer tolerate the abuse that God's people continued to experience, but now he had the clarity, direction and authority from God to do something about it. You see, he met with God Himself; he now knew the desert and the location of every watering hole and understood the terrain and the inherent challenges. The fact that Moses went through this exhaustive process ultimately made him one of God's most powerful leaders (and wilderness guides) and the one best suited to deliver His people from the grips of Egypt. Moses still had to work through the context of his own frail humanity. However, he could fully depend on God and His provisions in this new life-defining role. After all, this is how God receives the glory through our leadership.

In Exodus 15, we see an example of the transformation in Moses. The Hebrew people were in dire need of drinking water, but the waters before them were bitter. Moses could not resolve this with his 40 years of desert training! He understood his limitations as a leader and as a man, so he called on the one who could handle the situation – he cried out to God:

> *Then Moses led Israel from the Red Sea and they went into the Desert of Shur. For three days they traveled in the desert without finding water. When they came to Marah, they could not drink its water because it was bitter. (That is why the place is called Marah.[a]) So the people grumbled against Moses, saying, "What are we to drink?" Then Moses cried out to the Lord, and the Lord showed him a piece of wood [tree]. He threw it into the water, and the water became fit to drink.*

Exodus 15:22 - 25a

Though Moses knew the terrain and was aware of his
surroundings at that moment, God showed him a piece of wood
that had been there but escaped Moses' attention. This tree
became the tool God used to bring about the great miracle that
met the needs of His people. As with Moses, God wants to reveal
the natural things that have been primed for miraculous events in
our lives. He wants to show us new things that often escape our
understanding and vision. However, disobedience and the
embrace of sin and compromise can often keep us from seeing
and experiencing these wonderful moments. In Proverbs 29:18
we are reminded that *without vision we will be easily tripped-up by
temptation, fear, low self-esteem, indecision and more.*

Are you seeing the solutions and open doors that have been
placed in your life by God? The purpose, the gifts, resources, and
outright miracles are there – can you see them? Are you reaching
for these things? Or are you sulking in sorrow and pity, as you
once again shrink back from an opportunity to experience the
power of God in your life and in the life of those whom you
lead?

Where are you? Like so many of us, I wasted years in this
state of ambivalence and indecision. I was unsure where I stood,
and the power God wanted to offer me. This mindset affects our
sight and ability to hear God's voice.

I would pose to you that before you engage in any additional
leadership training, reading or conferences, you settle this with
God once and for all. What is stopping you? What is dragging
you down and keeping you from living the life you were designed
to live? Have you wondered if there is more for you? Do you
often ask, "Is this all He has for me?" The answer is NO!

God has more. Abundantly more. But you must surrender.
Make the decision to surrender your will and your plans – then

you will be positioned to embrace and experience His absolute best for you. If the obstacle is sin, then you can choose today, this very moment to drop that at His feet and experience the freedom that comes from Jesus.

Here's the good news. You're not surrendering to a God who only cares about what you bring to the table or what you can do for Him. He's committed to you first and your purpose second. Read what Ephesians 1:5-6 says to all who belong to Christ:

> *He predestined us to adoption as sons through Jesus Christ*
> *to Himself, according to the kind intention of His will,*
> *to the praise of the glory of His grace, which He freely*
> *bestowed on us in the Beloved.*

Did you know that in ancient Roman Law — a father could disown his biological son for practically any reason. The law made allowances for this act of abandonment. However, if you chose to adopt a child (legally), you could not undo that contract. You were bound for life. It was permanent! So now, when you read Ephesians 1:5-6, you should see it through the eyes of an adopted child who is confident in his or her father's "forever" commitment. You were called into this relationship and partnership with an eternal purpose and commitment that should give you the confidence to live life to the fullest. Don't hold back any longer, you have nothing to lose and everything to gain. You are part of His master plan. He says it in His Word and will be true to that covenant.

"D" is for Destiny. Would you embrace yours today? Give your heart and your future to God and surrender to His plan. You will never regret your journey. Take this moment now to rededicate your future, your gifts and purpose to Him. Then take your first step toward living the life He prepared for you!

"For we are God's handiwork (workmanship and

masterpiece), created in Christ Jesus to do good works, which God prepared in advance for us to do."

Ephesians 2:10

REFLECTION

What do you believe is the specific and unique purpose for your life? Can you describe it in one word? Can you describe it in one sentence?

_____

_____

_____

_____

_____

_____

_____

_____

_____

_____

Have you embraced your destiny and function in the body of Christ?

_____

_____

_____

_____

_____

_____

_____

_____

_____

What has been the biggest obstacle to achieving your purpose? What will you do to move forward today and this week? Create an action plan, and then call on a mentor to walk with you.

_____
_____
_____
_____
_____
_____
_____
_____
_____
_____
_____
_____
_____
_____
_____
_____
_____
_____
_____
_____
_____
_____
_____
_____
_____
_____
_____

5

The Burning Bush Event

*"The willingness to obey every word from God is
critical to hearing God speak."*
— *Henry T. Blackaby, Hearing God's Voice*

I love the story of Moses and his journey from Hebrew
infant, to Prince of Egypt, to desert shepherd, to deliverer
of God's people. What a journey! In an earlier chapter of
this book, we took a cursory look at the life and call of Moses.
There are many fascinating episodes in his story. But the one that
seems to capture most of our hearts and minds is that of the
"Burning Bush." While we already touched on this experience in
a prior chapter, I think that it merits a closer look. Why? Simply
stated, it represents a critical message to those of us called to
serve God's people:

Now Moses was tending the flock of Jethro his father-in-
law, the priest of Midian, and he led the flock to the
far side of the wilderness and came to Horeb, the
mountain of God. There the angel of the Lord
appeared to him in flames of fire from within a bush.
Moses saw that though the bush was on fire it did not
burn up. So Moses thought, "I will go over and see this
strange sight—why the bush does not burn up."
When the Lord saw that he had gone over to look, God
called to him from within the bush, "Moses! Moses!"
And Moses said, "Here I am."
"Do not come any closer," God said. "Take off your
sandals, for the place where you are standing is holy
ground." [6] *Then he said, "I am the God of your father,*
the God of Abraham, the God of Isaac and the God of
Jacob." At this, Moses hid his face, because he was
afraid to look at God.

Exodus 3: 1-6

As you consider this transformative voyage, you must also
consider the events as nothing less than miraculous. However, I
am sure that there were numerous instances during Moses' life
where things felt like anything but miraculous. Let's take a closer
look.

Chapter three comes into the picture approximately forty
years after his sudden and urgent departure from Egypt. I'd like
to park it there for a moment to share an observation. It is interesting to note that not much is said about his years in the desert.
Clearly God did a great deal of work in Moses during these years
in the desert. He must have experienced many trials, testing of
the heart and even the temptation to turn his back on God. This
is where Moses was able to process his first 40 years of life, and
his impulsive life-altering decision to kill an Egyptian man.

During this time, Moses interacted with the God of the Hebrew people. We can call this his time of God's "courting."

As with any relationship, the first steps are invested in learning about each other as well as sharing things about yourself that most people will not see. This is the time when people begin to know and understand each other. This is when we allow ourselves to become vulnerable in order to move a relationship into a deeper and more intimate level. This is where Moses found himself in the early years of his desert season.

During this time in the desert, all of the wisdom and knowledge that Moses gained while in Egypt was viewed through the filter of what I call "desert sequestration." In this place of desolation, all of Moses' "wrong" thoughts became "right." God Himself addressed all his questions. He had to confront his insecurities and fears and choose to trust God in all things. You see, there is no voice to hear other than the voice of God and your own when you are in the desert. Yet God chose to keep those details between Himself and His servant. I think that is quite admirable of our God. It speaks of His nature and character. This approach is similar to the story of other great men of God such as John the Baptist in the desert, and Paul in Arabia. They too experienced their own transformational journey. In His wisdom, God gives us only brief glimpses of these journeys and brings our attention to their entrance into their next stage of life. So why does God choose such an intimate and private approach to dealing with these men and with us? Perhaps the reason is that each of God's servants (each of us included) needs a unique and personal dealing whereby God is able to place His finger on the distinctive needs and disciplines suited for that individual. This is a personal work, and God honors that intimacy in all our lives. There is no place for a cookie cutter approach when God decides to deal with His masterpieces. Each one is precious and priceless – deserving of a personal touch from His loving hands.

When we arrive at the third chapter of Exodus, Moses comes

across a bush that is set ablaze. According to botanists, there are certain plants that contain gaseous pods or oil glands that could have explained the seemingly endless flame. However, after forty years in the desert Moses would have recognized something that was natural, and may I say, nondescript. It is safe to also surmise that Moses was accustomed to seeing many desert fires. In the intense heat of the desert sun, I am sure that there were occasions when he saw many brush fires in response to the heat or neglect of men traveling through the desert. This fire was so unusual and out of the normal boundaries of his experience that it aroused his curiosity and compelled him to move toward further examination.

When Moses drew closer to the burning bush, he realized that it was not being consumed. How is that possible? That goes against the laws of nature and common sense. Some have tried to explain this phenomenon away by saying that this particular bush was located over a volcanic area of the desert and therefore, the ongoing flame could be easily explained. However, it doesn't explain how the intense heat and flames did not consume the bush.

When God chose to speak to Moses, His supernatural presence enveloped that area and the bush responded in the natural by burning. Now, the miraculous took on a greater manifestation, as the bush would not disintegrate into a heap of ashes. You see, when God descended into time and space in order to speak to His servant Moses, he brought into our finite world His immutable DNA and character. What does it mean when I say that He is "immutable?"

The Immutability of God is an attribute where "God is unchanging in his character, will, and covenant promises." The Westminster Shorter Catechism says, "God is a spirit, whose being, wisdom power, holiness, justice, goodness, and truth are infinite, eternal, and unchangeable." Those things do not change.

Going further, Webster's Dictionary defines 'immutable' as "not capable of or susceptible to change."

The Bible also corroborates this finding; following are two verses that clearly portray God's immutable character and nature:

> *"Because God wanted to make the unchanging nature of his purpose very clear to the heirs of what was promised, he confirmed it with an oath."[1]*

Hebrews 6:17

> *"I the Lord do not change. So you, the descendants of Jacob, are not destroyed."*

Malachi 3:6

Why am I investing so much into this point? I am glad you asked! If God's immutable nature affected "the burning bush" so that it was not consumed, how do you think that His immutable nature will affect the call and purpose on your life? Ephesians 2:10 says,

> *"For we are God's handiwork, created in Christ Jesus to do good works, which God prepared in advance for us to do."*

If that is the case and God is immutable, then we can safely conclude that His plan for us will stand no matter the obstacle or natural explanation for its termination.

"Well John, you don't know how I have failed God over the years. You have no idea how I have wasted so many years. God's plan for my life must have been annulled by now." You might say.

To that I would respond, "You are correct. I don't know how you have failed God." But I would also say, "You are also wrong."

If God is immutable, so is His plan for you! Consequently, there is nothing that you or I can do to cause God to change His vision and plan. There is nothing that you can say or do that will place you outside of His reach. You have been redeemed for such a great purpose. You are precious to His heart and integral to His plan. This principle is clearly conveyed in Romans 11:29 where we read, "For the gifts and calling of God are without repentance." So just as the bush did not burn and turn into a heap of dust because of God's DNA, neither will your call and purpose as a leader. His DNA flows through you because of His Holy Spirit.

We see this wellspring shared in 2 Timothy 1:14:

"Guard, through the Holy Spirit who dwells in us, the treasure which has been entrusted to you."

We also see similar evidence in Ezekiel 36:27, where it says,

"I will put My Spirit within you and cause you to walk in My statutes, and you will be careful to observe My ordinances."[2]

His call is draped over you. Why then would your purpose not stand the test of time? Too often we heed the lies of the enemy and ignore God's promises and faithfulness. In order to experience all that He has for us, we must close sensory receptors to the voice of defeat and decide to only receive from God and those called to minister to us during this season. As we do this, we are then positioned to respond to His call and His plan.

We've discussed this burning bush quite a bit. So now we should consider how Moses responded to the burning bush. Chapter 3 sheds light on an important life lesson that all leaders should embrace. Moses saw the fire from afar and decided to draw closer. So many of us see something in our horizon, but rather than walking toward that thing and inspecting, we remain far-off, often aloof wondering, "What could that be? Could that be for me?" As we do this, we wonder why God doesn't respond to our questions or contemplation. The answer is simple. He will only speak the details into our lives when we approach Him with an open and pure heart.

Truth be told, God rarely shouts at His children, "Do this!" "Go there!" "Start here!" He usually whispers His instructions and desires. He does this to ensure intimacy and proper proximity. If He whispers, then you and I must draw near to Him in order to listen and receive His message.

No one listens to a whisper from across the room. That is why, I believe, Moses was drawn to the burning bush. I believe that his compulsion to further explore this oddity was in fact his spirit responding to the whisper of his God – El Roi, the God who saw him in the desert.

You will notice that this is precisely what the Lord did with Moses. He did not speak until He saw that Moses' eyes and full attention were fixed on the burning bush – on Him. Scripture reads as follows:

> *"When the Lord saw that he had gone over to look, God called to him from within the bush, "Moses! Moses!"*

Exodus 3:4

This speaks to God's intimate and personal nature. While He is more than capable to yell from a distance, He clearly prefers close encounters. I believe that He does this for our benefit and advancement. He knows that our propensity is to explain away things that are supernatural. The further you are from a supernatural event, the easier it will be to dismiss. However, if you approach and remain close, then you are positioned for a miraculous encounter. You will be challenged if you attempt to shelve or ignore the message.

God is looking for men and women who are not afraid to walk toward His voice. He is in search of those who will not allow life's distractions, hurts and disappointments to keep them from the face-to-face moments that are designed to change the trajectory of their lives. He is also looking for servant leaders who are open to an intimate relationship with Him. Do you want to feel His soft breath on your face? Do you long for that intimacy with the Father?

As you read Exodus 3:4, you see that the Lord concludes His call by repeating Moses' name twice. Why is that significant? This is one of those things that can be easily disregarded unless you understand what a repeated name means in the Jewish culture. It is an expression of intimacy and closeness reserved to those who are in the inner circle of the one calling. In Scripture, we see a number of instances where this is recorded. We see this when the Lord speaks to Abraham on Mount Moriah, as he is about to sacrifice his son Isaac. We also see this when God instructs Jacob to go on his journey to Egypt and when He first called young Samuel. Jesus also employed this same expression of intimacy when He confronted Martha and when He cautioned Peter, and let's not forget when Jesus wept over Jerusalem. In all of these cases, we find names repeated as profound expressions of intimacy.

As leaders we must seek that intimate place in our relationship and journey with the Lord, as that will be where revelation and clarity is found. There are those who pretend to have an intimate relationship with the Lord, but this is not reflected in their walk or service. The Bible clearly warns us to not be like those who say, "Lord, Lord," but live in contempt for His commands –

"If you love me, keep my commands. And I will ask the

Father, and he will give you another advocate to help
you and be with you forever".

John 14:15

Your pursuit of this intimacy and closeness to Jesus will produce a likeness to Him that will elevate your ministry in ways that no seminar or degree can ever realize. That is the missing link in most ministries. There may be great fanfare, expertise and amazing production quality, but the nearness and sense of Jesus is absent. Do not omit that ingredient from your life and ministry. Take the time to hear His voice in the desert and walk toward your personal burning bush. There is no need to fear that experience. What you will find there will become a defining mark in your life. You will never be the same.

REFLECTION

Can you identify a "burning bush" event in your life?

_____

_____

_____

_____

_____

_____

_____

_____

_____

_____

_____

How would you describe your level of intimacy with God?

_____

_____

_____

_____

_____

_____

_____

_____

_____

_____

_____

How do you practice intimacy with God? Has this approach been effective for your growth and understanding of His heart?

_____

_____

_____

_____

_____

_____

_____

_____

_____

_____

_____

_____

_____

_____

_____

_____

_____

_____

_____

_____

_____

_____

_____

1. Both scripture references here come from the New International Version of the Bible.
2. NIV

6

Advance

"To have found God and still to pursue Him is the soul's paradox of love."
— *A. W. Tozer, The Pursuit of God*

The Bible is filled with abundant life and leadership lessons. One of my favorite examples is found in the book of 2 Timothy. This book is known as Paul's final letter, and it is addressed to his closest companion and protégé - Timothy. Although the Apostle could have settled on his own accomplishments, he is more interested in making sure that Timothy is prepared to carry on the work of the Lord. The two themes seen throughout this letter are "endurance" and "faithfulness," as it relates to scriptural truth and its transformative power. These themes might be summarized in this manner: "Persevere in the proclamation of the Gospel." While Paul is in prison, he is still fixed on advancing the cause of Jesus Christ. His life and work might be nearing its end, but the mission itself is far from over. Pause, and take that in for a moment.

So how do we, as leaders, move forward in our purpose and also move His purpose forward – regardless of adverse circumstances, obstacles and perhaps risk of substantial loss? Let's examine 2 Timothy 3:14-17.[1]

> *"But as for you, **continue** (menó [men'-o]: to stay in a given place, state, relation or expectancy -- abide, dwell, endure, be present, remain, stand, tarry) in what you have learned and have become convinced of, because you know those from whom you learned it, and how from infancy you have known the Holy Scriptures, which are able to make you wise for salvation through faith in Christ Jesus. All Scripture is God-breathed and is useful for teaching, rebuking, correcting and training in righteousness, so that the servant of God may be **thoroughly equipped** (exartizó [ex-ar-tid'-zo] completely furnish, finish) for every good work."*

God created you for a purpose. He gifted you with undeniable abilities and talents. He expects you to share them with others. All you have to do is discover your calling – and then show up for it each day. The rest is up to Him! There are practical steps that we must take in order to experience this purpose and journey. That is what Paul was consistently communicating to the believers in the early church as noted below:

Philippians 1:6 says,

> *"For I am confident of this very thing, that He who began a good work in you will perfect it until the day of Christ Jesus."*

God is faithful to finish, but we must be present, and active participants. In this chapter, we will go over several useful principles that we must "gain" to ensure that we are positioned to "advance" our purpose and His kingdom. Feel free to scribble some notes around each section so that you can consider and apply them to your unique leadership journey:

1. We must gain a radical attitude toward sin because it is deceitful.

> *"See to it, brothers and sisters, that none of you has a*
> *sinful, unbelieving heart that turns away from the*
> *living God. But encourage one another daily, as long as*
> *it is called 'Today,' so that none of you may be*
> ***hardened*** *by sin's deceitfulness."*
>
> Hebrews 3:12-13

The word for "hardened" is the word from which we get "sclerosis". What is sclerosis? It is a gradual hardening of something – arteries, nervous system, etc. In the picture that I just presented to you exists a grave consequence. In the process of hardening, we experience a *decreased* sensitivity and receptiveness to movement of any kind. For example, when a person suffers from multiple sclerosis, the areas of the body affected by this disease are no longer able to effectively respond to the messages sent by the brain through its intended channels of the nervous system.

Likewise, if we experience spiritual sclerosis, we will be unable to receive important directives from the Lord through His Holy Spirit. With that said, if we fail to respond radically against sin we will drift because it is deceitful. Some time ago, I came across a quite unsettling, but powerful illustration about sin that will help bring this point across. This illustration is called, "How an Eskimo Kills a Wolf."

Here we go…

In Alaska, many people live off the land. They grow crops and also hunt for their daily sustenance. Given that some Eskimos live in the thick of the wilderness, they must employ survival tactics used by prior generations. Once an animal is killed and prepared for cooking later that day or the next day, it is often left hanging outside because the frigid weather ensures that the meat remains frozen and well preserved. Unfortunately, the wilderness presents many challenges – namely, hungry wolf packs. With their keen sense of smell, they are able to locate a frozen carcass miles away. On occasions, wolves will find meat that is hung by an Eskimo and will ravage it well before the Eskimo returns to recover his meal.

One remedy that has been passed-on through generations is a sure way to end this dilemma. The Eskimo takes several sharp knives, coats the blades with animal blood and allows the blood to freeze on the blade. He proceeds to add another layer, then another, and yet another, until the blades are completely concealed by a thick coat of frozen blood. He then secures the handles of the knives in the frozen ground throughout his property. In doing so, his food is surrounded by the sharp, blood-covered blades protruding from the ground. When the hungry wolves return to the Eskimo's property later that evening, their keen sense of smell attracts them to the knives and they begin to lick the frozen blood covering the blades on the ground, completely ignoring the hanging carcasses belonging to the Eskimo family.

Their hunger and thirst for blood entices them to lick the blood-covered blades faster and faster until they reach a state of frenzied feeding. At this point, the frozen blood has been consumed and the wolves begin to lick their own warm blood as they cut their tongues on the now exposed blades. They don't notice that their own warm blood is now the thing satisfying their blood lust. They continue on to their own demise. Yes, this is a graphic scene, but so is the end result of unfettered sin in our lives.

The thirst for sin will never be quenched in the natural. Sin ultimately leads to the demise of the person who is its slave. That is why the Bible clearly and uncompromisingly tells us that we are to radically and fiercely confront any sin that resides in our lives. We are then called to live in holiness (set apart) and in alignment with God.

> *"But just as He who called you is holy, so be holy in all*
> *you do; for it is written: Be holy, because I am holy."*

> 1 Peter 1:15-16

God calls us to be holy so that as we do, we are able to take-on His DNA, His heart, and vision for life. Sin distorts our view of life and disables our ability to hear His voice. Even if we approach God with sincere hearts, we are unable to hear clearly because sin separates us and keeps us from drawing near enough to hear His response to our cry. To achieve this, the leader must be courageous and not intimidated by the aching consequences of turning his back on sin. We have a great example of this in Daniel 3:16-18:

> *Shadrach, Meshach and Abednego replied to him, "King*
> *Nebuchadnezzar, we do not need to defend ourselves*
> *before you in this matter. If we are thrown into the*
> *blazing furnace, the God we serve is able to deliver us*
> *from it, and he will deliver us from Your Majesty's*
> *hand. But even if he does not, we want you to know,*
> *Your Majesty, that we will not serve your gods or*
> *worship the image of gold you have set up."*

They were determined to stay the course of purity and

commitment to what they knew would please God — even if it led
to their cruel and dreadful demise in a fiery furnace. This may
sound like a boxing or MMA match:

(The Champion) Life in Christ -vs- (The Challenger) indulging
in Sin.

It truly is a fight, but one worth engaging in, as it will further
align you with God and His plan for your life. If you continually
vacillate by fighting one day, then indulging the next in whatever
your flesh desires, then you will be like the crashing wave that
aimlessly goes back and forth. Here is what Scripture says:

> *"Then we will no longer be infants, tossed back and forth*
> *by the waves, and blown here and there by every wind*
> *of teaching and by the cunning and craftiness of people*
> *in their deceitful scheming. Instead, speaking the truth*
> *in love, we will grow to become in every respect the*
> *mature body of him who is the head, that is, Christ."*

Ephesians 4:14-15

Leaders must become the "mature body of Jesus who is the
head. Unfortunately, there is no magic pill. This is a battle that
requires your involvement. No hiding or running the other way.
Sin must be confronted head-on and eradicated from your life.
Now, I am not saying that you will be "sinless." We can all
agree that we will reach that status in heaven and heaven only.
Until then, we are to avoid practicing or continuously living in
a state of sin. We are to avoid sinful thoughts and practices that
should not reside in our daily walk. That is what God desires
of us. He has made a way for us to live our days set apart and
in communion with Him, through His Holy Spirit. The Bible
tells us that we have all we need for godly living — we must

simply grab hold of it today and experience what He has for us:

"His divine power has given us everything we need for a godly life through our knowledge of him who called us by his own glory and goodness."

2 Peter 1:3

2. Gain understanding of God's Word.

Both the Old and New Testaments are relevant to our lives; they were given to help us move ahead in our purpose and journey with the Lord. Some believers may have a greater affinity toward one Testament over the other, but truth be told, the entire canon of Scripture is God's Word, and it exists in perfect harmony. This is why it is so important that leaders embrace the entire Word of God and apply it in its entirety - with balance and understanding. In doing so the leader is empowered to receive sound counsel from the Lord as it relates to the daily challenges of life. Following are some interesting facts about Scripture that demonstrate the value of one testament to the other:

- An index in the Jewish New Testament catalogs *695 separate quotations* from the books of the Old Testament in the New. *(Jewish New Testament Publications, Jerusalem, 1989)*
- The number of quotations and references in the New Testament to the Old may be as high as *4,105.* (Roger Nicole, 1979).
- The apostles quoted the Old Testament *695 times,* but other writers *only four times.*
- Of the 26 books and letters forming the New Testament, 20 quote the Old Testament.

- There are 39 books in the Old Testament. Of these thirty-nine books, only nine are not quoted in the New Testament.
- The five books of Moses are quoted at least *245 times* and referred to many more times than that.
- Paul, the apostle who some believe taught that the law contained in these five books was done away with, quoted from those books between *70 and 110 times* more than any other New Testament figure.
- Jesus Christ quoted from the same books about 60 times.

Here is what Scripture has to say about the importance of its words in our lives:

> *"Keep this Book of the Law always on your lips; meditate on it day and night, so that you may be careful to do everything written in it. Then you will be prosperous and successful."*[2]

> *"Your word is a lamp for my feet, a light on my path."*[3]

> *"For the Word that God speaks is alive and full of power [making it active, operative, energizing, and effective]; it is sharper than any two-edged sword, penetrating to the dividing line of the breath of life (soul) and [the immortal] spirit, and of joints and marrow [of the deepest parts of our nature], exposing and sifting and analyzing and judging the very thoughts and purposes of the heart."*[4]

Even though we understand the importance of God's Word in our lives, the sad reality is that the Bible has become a rare commodity in the Christian community. This is also reflected among many leaders – big and small. We have become a society led by popular opinion, Christianized self-help principles, statements from preachers on television, social media, and quick Internet searches.

Someone once said, "Leaders are readers." I wholeheartedly agree with that statement. Schedule the time throughout your days to read great books on leadership and Christian living. There are many amazing books you can purchase on-line. However, do not overlook the importance of reading the Bible for yourself; it will become your barometer and gauge for godly living and sound leadership – grounded in wisdom from heaven.

> *"Reading sweeps the cobwebs away; it increases our power of concentration; it makes us more interesting to be around; and it strengthens our ability to glean truth from God's Word. Even in prison, Paul wanted his books, especially the parchments (2 Timothy 4:13) brought to him. He would have agreed with John Wesley who said, "Either read or get out of ministry!"*
>
> - Charles R. Swindoll, Come Before Winter.

3. Gain discipline.

"Before you can conquer the world, you must first conquer self." - Plato

In 1 Timothy 3:2-7, Paul explains to Timothy the requirements and disciplines of an overseer or leader in the church. Let's take a close look at some of the highlights found in Paul's message:

- Lazy and disorganized people never rise to true leadership.
- Many who aspire to leadership, at home and

elsewhere, fail because they have never learned to follow.

- Godly control of the secret place prepares the stage for public victory and authority.

A proven leader will be one who consistently reads the Word of God, applies it in his or her daily life, and then lives out a standard before all so that they in turn may follow.

Apathetic leaders who refuse to implement the lessons gleaned from Scripture become impotent and ineffective. This is not how we transform the world. For too long, we have seen this play out on the grand stage of Christendom, and now is the time to eradicate this practice of apathy from our churches and ministries. God is seeking men and women who will seek Him in Spirit and in truth. Will that be you?

4. Gain understanding - A godly leader must have insight and vision into spiritual things.

I would like to begin this point by examining the definition of "insight," as I believe it will help us better understand our objective in this area of growth:

- The power or act of seeing into a situation: penetration
- The act or result of apprehending the inner nature of things or of seeing intuitively

A leader who lacks insight is one who is misinformed and sadly ill equipped to lead a ministry or group into battle or even an opportunity. You see, without insight, the leader lacks the lay of the land that he or she is called to conquer. Without insight, a leader is limited in his or her ability to set a course of action. I would liken this to mountain climbers who decide to traverse the tallest mountain in the world with no guides. That choice would most likely result in death.

Almost everyone considers Mount Everest "the highest mountain in the world," and climbers from all parts of the world travel to Everest hoping to earn the distinction of climbing the "World's Highest Mountain." Mount Everest rises 29,035 feet above sea level. No other mountain on Earth has a higher altitude.

Over the years many have attempted to climb Mount Everest and have either failed and retreated, or sadly met their demise on the frozen elevations of this colossal mountain. For that reason, many have employed the support of "Sherpas."

These Sherpas are typically men who are members of a Himalayan people living on the borders of Nepal and Tibet, renowned for their skill in mountaineering. These men have lived their lives at high altitude and have insight and understanding of that unique and rugged topography. As such, they are uniquely positioned to lead others up the side of the mountain until they reach the summit. This is not something you can learn in school. It is a skill earned through years of exposure and experience.

I once read a story about, Pemba Gyalje Sherpa who was part of the group of climbers who, in early August 2008, began the last leg of their summit of K2, a mountain in the heart of the Karakoram Range in northern Pakistan. At 28,251 feet, K2 is second in height only to Everest, but its peak is even steeper, colder and more desolate than its Himalayan sister.

On that journey, eleven climbers lost their lives, nine of them after an ice pillar severed the fixed ropes, they needed to retreat down an icy chute called the Bottleneck. It was Pemba Gyalje Sherpa who rescued two of the climbers who were trapped above 26,000 feet, where oxygen is scarce. When he returned to his home in Katmandu, Nepal, he said his family and friends pleaded with him to stop mountaineering. "But climbing and guiding is my life," he said, "and I will never stop." The next season, he was back on the mountain, leading expeditions of the Himalayas.

In like fashion, as a leader, you must possess the drive and passion exhibited by Mr. Sherpa. You must also have a keen understanding of the terrain before leading people up the proverbial summit. Anything less than that will create an environment of loss and casualty for your team and organization.

In addition to the above attributes and skills, the leader must have "vision." In definition they must have a (1): *mode of seeing or conceiving* (2): *unusual discernment or foresight.*

As a leader, you must see your purpose beyond your immediate surroundings and reality. Leadership vision allows you to set the course and navigation for those who lack foresight, but who are still able to follow and grow under those who have it.

Since there are those who may have limited vision and understanding, you must fine-tune your vision to see how your decisions today will affect you and future generations. So how do you achieve this vantage point? The first thing you must do is read God's Word, and second, you must spend quality and consistent time in prayer. Ultimately, it is His vision and plan that you need for yourself and those whom you lead. Therefore, these two ingredients; the Bible and prayer, are vital to anything you say or do in your role as leader.

Lastly, vision involves optimism and hope. "The leader who sees the difficulties so clearly that he or she does not discern the possibilities cannot *inspire* a vision in others."[5] Consequently, no matter what you see before you as a leader, you must be able to see beyond limitations and obstacles. You must also see the potential and motivate those around you to see it as well.

5. Gain wisdom; if knowledge comes by study, wisdom comes by way of the Holy Spirit.

Paul's prayer for the Christians in Colossians 1:9 should be our own: [*Personalized*] *"God fill me with the knowledge of Your will through all spiritual wisdom and understanding."*

So, for the sake of this discussion, let us explore the concept of wisdom and its application according to Scripture. What better example than that of young Solomon and his pursuit of wisdom. This story, in the Bible, speaks of Solomon after God offered him anything his heart desired. Amazingly, Solomon requested wisdom over power, riches and fame. In response to his humble wish, God said to Solomon:

> *"Because this was in your heart, and you have not asked*
> *riches or wealth or honor or the life of your enemies, nor*
> *have you asked long life—but have asked wisdom and*
> *knowledge for yourself, that you may judge My people*
> *over whom I have made you king— wisdom and*
> *knowledge are granted to you; and I will give you riches*
> *and wealth and honor, such as none of the kings have*
> *had who were before you, nor shall any after you have*
> *the like."*[6]

Whether or not you are a leader there is so much to be gained from this powerful story. The Webster's Unabridged Dictionary defines wisdom as *"knowledge, and the capacity to make due use of it."* Let's take a look at some of the attributes of wisdom in the life of a leader:

- Wisdom gives a leader balance and helps to avoid extremes that lead to compromise and ineffectiveness. Ecclesiastes 2:13 – *"And I realized that there is an advantage to wisdom over folly, like the advantage of light over darkness."*
- Wisdom is insight into the heart of God. James 3:17 – *"But the wisdom from above is first pure, then peaceable, gentle, reasonable, full of mercy and good fruits, unwavering, without hypocrisy."*

- Wisdom is a prerequisite to lead and to follow. Acts 6:3 – *"Brothers and sisters, choose seven men from among you who are known to be full of the Spirit and wisdom. We will turn this responsibility over to them."*

The attainment of wisdom is vital in the life of a leader. But it is also a key ingredient in the life of anyone who wishes to live a fruitful and well-adjusted life. The fruit of this pursuit is not attained by magic that comes to some and skips others. There is no magic spell or genie in a bottle. If you desire wisdom, all you must do is simply make the choice to become an open and willing vessel. You must also be prepared to practice the wisdom that is imparted to you by Scripture and those placed over you in life by God.

Charles Spurgeon once said, *"Wisdom is the right use of knowledge. To know is not to be wise. Many men know a great deal and are all the greater fools for it. There is no fool so great a fool as a knowing fool."*

6. Gain the ability to decide; the godly leader will not vacillate when faced with a decision, nor after making it.

In the book of James, we find a portion of Scripture that has been used many times through the annals of the church. Unfortunately, Christians and many leaders have not embraced it to the extent that it warrants. This familiar verse simply states,

"But when you ask, you must believe and not doubt, because the one who doubts is like a wave of the sea, blown and tossed by the wind. That person should not expect to receive anything from the Lord. Such a person is double-minded and unstable in all they do."

James 1:6-9

Following are three points to consider on the matter of vacillation and procrastination:

- Don't be quick to declare your preference or path before you have all the information on hand and before you have lingered in God's presence. A leader must weigh evidence and make his or her decisions on sound biblical grounds. False starts and backtracking create confusion and disillusionment in the hearts of those who are standing with you. Waiting on God will never delay your plans. His green light is always timely.

- Once assured of God's will, a leader must be prepared to spring into action without fear of consequences. The Bible is replete with examples of this principle. One such story is found in Genesis 14; this is when Abraham rescued his nephew Lot from the kings who attacked Sodom. He didn't mull it over as he reviewed a list of benefits and liabilities. As soon as he knew that God instructed him to go, he simply obeyed. Debating with God's directives leads to a weakening of your faith. It also creates an environment of fear and doubt. When you hear the word, "go," simply do as the Lord tells you. He has never missed the mark.

- When presented with a choice between the pleasures of Egypt and the sufferings of leading God's people, Moses decided to follow his destiny.[7] Sometimes the choices are crystal clear, yet the price can easily dissuade you as a leader. Don't allow that to happen, as you will miss out on the great plan of God over your life. I often remind my sons and young leaders that, "the greatest pain is the pain of regret." Don't

allow yourself to miss out on the opportunity to act on
behalf of the God of Heaven!

Charles H. Spurgeon once said, *"Lives with many aims are like
water trickling through innumerable streams, none of which are wide enough
or deep enough to float the merest cockleshell of a boat; but a life with one
object is like a mighty river flowing between its banks, bearing to the ocean a
multitude of ships, and spreading fertility on either side."* Like that river,
God's leader will choose His lane and with a single-minded
resolve realize God's purpose.

**7. Gain courage; leaders require courage of the highest
order – always moral and at times physical.**

One of my favorite Scriptures on courage is found in
Deuteronomy 31:6. It says,

> *"Be strong and of good courage, do not fear nor be afraid
> of them; for the Lord your God, He is the One who
> goes with you. He will not leave you nor forsake you."*

As you read this verse, you can immediately see the structure
of a call to a courageous life - as one who completely relies on an
almighty God. Like the good father that He is, God is saying here
that He will accompany us, and then proceeds to reassure us by
saying that He will not leave nor forsake us. So, the moral of this
story is that, our courage should not be based on our strength or
ability, but rather on God. Now that is what I call a great deal!

Following are a few additional morsels for you to consume on
this important topic:

- The Apostle Paul admitted to knowing fear, but it
  never stopped him. 1 Corinthians 2:3 *"I came to you in
  weakness and fear, and with much trembling."* The point

here is that even if you encounter fear or intimidation, in an area of your leadership, *"do it afraid."* Do not allow fear to be a period in your life's mission statement. It may be a comma, but never a period. Don't give fear the final say in your journey. Moreover, never allow 'man' to keep you from God's decree over you.

- Before his death Martin Luther said, *"I was afraid of nothing; God can make one so desperately bold."* This man understood God's statement in Deuteronomy 31:6; "Be strong and courageous. Do not be afraid or terrified because of them, for the Lord your God goes with you; he will never leave you nor forsake you." He understood that the Lord was with him – always.

- All leaders must face their fears as they move forward. John 20:19 tells us, *"The doors were locked for fear of the Jews."* The Disciples had not yet faced their new reality following the death of their beloved master – Jesus. As a result, they cowered in anticipation of their own demise. They had placed all their hope in this one man who, as far as they knew, was no longer alive. Everything they believed now hung on the balance of belief and unbelief. Thankfully, their Messiah revealed Himself and brought life to their faith and their courage so that they could carry on with the work that awaited them. Nonetheless, they had a decision to make— to march past fear and the reality of what they might encounter. Thankfully, they embraced courage and became the vehicle that God used to continue promoting the message of salvation through Jesus Christ.

Through the power of the Holy Spirit, those whom you lead and serve will see and experience your courage. As you take a

stand for truth, your deeds will speak volumes to those around
you. This will become foundational to your impact and influence
on the lives of those whom you lead. A great example of this is
found in Acts 4:13. In this portion of Scripture, the religious
leaders took note of the courage found in Peter and John. The
fact was irrefutable: *"When they saw the courage of Peter and John and
realized that they were unschooled, ordinary men, they were astonished, and
they took note that these men had been with Jesus."* Can the same be said
of you and me? May the answer be a resounding yes!

8. Gain humility; it is the hallmark of a spiritual leader.

> *"It is not humility to underrate yourself. Humility is to
> think of yourself as God thinks of you. It is to feel that
> if we have talents God has given them to us. And let it
> be seen that, like freight in a vessel, they tend to sink us
> low. The more we have, the lower we ought to lie."*
>
> Charles Spurgeon

Far too often, leaders will associate humility with weakness.
As a result, many will gravitate to a polar opposite in an effort to
salvage their name and reputation. This has hindered and
delayed many leaders from experiencing God's best for them and
those who follow them.

In Matthew 20:25-27, Jesus himself told His disciples to avoid
the ostentatious attitudes of the gentile rulers. He knew that this
would hurt their ability to grow in their roles as leaders of the
church. Jesus instructed and modeled this behavior so that spiritual men and women would choose the hidden path of sacrificial
service and approval of the Lord over the accolades of man. The
Apostle Paul also exemplified this lifestyle as he too followed Jesus
after his conversion. We see this in the following Scripture verses:

"For I am the least of the apostles and do not even deserve to be called an apostle, because I persecuted the church of God."

1 Corinthians 15:9

We should also consider 1 Timothy 1:15:

"Here is a trustworthy saying that deserves full acceptance: Christ Jesus came into the world to save sinners—of whom I am the worst."

As leaders, we can no longer afford to undervalue the significance of humility in our service. The stage is set for leaders to do their work with one primary purpose. We are to ensure that all things point to Jesus first and foremost. Sadly, today we see a trend toward celebrity pastors and Christian leaders who have taken on the persona of rock stars rather than servants doing the work of the Lord. Hear me my friend; that is a trap and will destroy you, your ministry, and the lives of those around you. Remain grounded as a servant leader and deflect all compliments and accolades to the One who deserves all attention, and His name is Jesus. Following are several tips that will help you remain focused as a humble servant-leader:

- Study God's Word for yourself and remain open to guidance. - Proverbs 3:5-8
- Offer your gifts to God and serve with a heart of sacrifice. - Romans 12:1-21
- Be quick to confess, forgive and ask for forgiveness. - 1 John 1:9
- Be a good follower that is faithful, truthful, supportive and encouraging to the leadership - 1 Corinthians 13:4-8

- Be quick to hear, slow to speak and slow to anger – this is so very important! - James 1:19
- Always look to Jesus and His cross. - Mark 10:45
- Remain accountable to those over you in ministry. - Ecclesiastes 4:9-12

Relentlessly focus - The principles shared in this chapter will lead to consistent victory and effectiveness in your life as you move forward to advance His purpose. Take time to examine your life in light of these principles and ask the Lord to show you how to proceed. Begin with the reflection section below, but don't stop there. Examine, reflect, and then find a trustworthy mentor to serve as your sounding board. It is time to grow. It is time to lead. Ready? Set? Go!

REFLECTION

How has your attitude toward sin helped or hindered your leadership journey?

_____

_____

_____

_____

_____

_____

_____

_____

In John 20:19, we see how fear affected the Disciples. How has fear affected you in recent days? How have you countered that, and what Scripture have you employed to keep you moving forward? If you have not recently dealt with fear, find the Scripture you would share with another leader facing insurmountable fear.

_____

_____

_____

_____

_____

_____

_____

_____

_____

Do you have an accountability partner or system in place? If not, make it a priority today to ask the Lord to show you that person who will walk along side you. This is essential if you wish to enjoy a long and effective ministry.

_____

1. NIV   with emphasis added
2. Joshua 1:8
3. Psalm 119:105
4. Hebrews 4:12 AMP
5. J. Oswald Sanders
6. 2 Chronicles 1:11-12, NKJV
7. Hebrews 11:24

Running on Empty - The Dangers of a Prayerless Life

*"Walking with God down the avenues of prayer we acquire
something of His likeness, and unconsciously we become witnesses
to others of His beauty and His grace."*
— E. M. Bounds

As we read Zechariah 1:1-6, we encounter a young
prophet who entered the scene during the building of
the temple. Other great prophets and leaders who were
also used by God lived during this time: Haggai, Zerubbabel,
Nehemiah and Ezra. During this great undertaking, we see the
power that is made available when God's people engage with
Him. God's people needed and received both encouragement
and correction through the prophet Zechariah so that they would
return to the Lord and complete the work that was before them.

There is a similar call to God's people today – especially leaders. Many of us have drifted into a lifestyle of prayerlessness. This has moved us to a mode of operation where our abilities, gifts, networks and possessions have become our source in ministry and life. Too often, leaders will refer to what the famous pastors on social media are doing. They will "borrow" sermons and will insistently imitate, rather than go before the Father in prayer for inspiration, leading and anointing.

As a result of this insatiable dependence on man, I have met far too many Pastors and leaders who now lead in fear, uncertainty, and complacency. Some time ago, I watched a riveting video illustration that bolstered the point of how we use our time. Following is a breakdown of that illustration. It will help us to see why so many leaders find themselves in this quandary of fear and confusion - *"40 Million Minutes."*

Let's take a moment to review the following facts:

1. The average person lives 77 years. That equates to 28,000 days, 670,000 hours, or 40 million minutes.
2. The average person spends 24 minutes a day getting dressed. That equals 13 hours a month, 7 days a year, or 1 year in a lifetime.
3. The average person spends 40 minutes a day on the phone. That factors out to 20 hours a month, 10 days a year, or 2 years in a lifetime. This number has grown exponentially in recent years, so we can only imagine what this number would be now!
4. The average person spends 3 hours a day watching television. That's 90 hours a month, 45 days a year, and 9 years in a lifetime.
5. Then the video presents this captivating fact. The average Christian spends less than 10 minutes a day in prayer. That equates to less than 6 hours a month, 3 days a year, and 7 months in a lifetime. The video ends with this line: "You do the math."

Take a moment right now and allow these numbers to sink into your heart and mind. Now, I will ask you, "Do these numbers reflect your current reality?" I challenge you to write your answer beside this paragraph along with today's date. Use this as a reminder and impetus for change.

As we think about these findings, we can easily see why the average church; the average Christian; the average leader is just that... AVERAGE.

Someone once asked, if you or your church were to suddenly "disappear" from your community, would anyone notice? Would it affect the course of life for anyone? Would people have to read-just, or would anyone even notice?

I too had to face this reality in my journey as a Christian and leader. On an average day, I would relegate my "time with the Lord" during the drive to the office or a meeting. Even then, the prayers would be lifeless and routine. I could have recorded the prayer and requests and simply hit the "play" button. Thankfully, the time came when I realized that it was simply not enough.

Today, I continue to grow in this area of my relationship with the Lord. I allocate my time with the Lord as the first fruit of my day. My daily goal is to spend quality time in prayer, quite medi-tation and the Word. You will find your own "formula", but I often start my time in worship. I sit in my home office and play worship music, sing along or simply begin to worship Him and invite Him into my space. I then take some time to pray for my loved ones, special prayer requests and needs. At this juncture in my relationship, I trust Him enough where I don't linger too much asking Him to "do this" or "touch this situation." I trust Him enough to know that He has all things under control. During this time, I simply acknowledge that I know He is working on my behalf and those in my life. I also use this time to thank Him for things He's done and even thank Him in advance for things that I believe He will do. He's a good father, so I trust Him.

The one thing that I have recently incorporated into my prayer time is sitting silently in His presence. This has been a tough discipline for me. My mind is often racing ahead thinking of the thousands of things that I must do later that day. Yet, as I have trained my heart and mind to sit silently before Him, I have learned so much about Him and myself. You see, how else will we hear His voice if we don't make the time to listen?

God is always speaking; however, his children do not always make the time to listen. As a result, this has become a priority in my life. Every day, I close my prayer time by saying, "Speak to me Lord, your servant is listening." Then I sit silently and peacefully. I don't always hear or sense His voice at that moment. However, many times during the course of the day, I will hear His voice in my heart and mind speaking peace, direction and even providing wisdom. You see, He speaks when He is ready to speak. Remain vigilant with ears attuned to His sweet soft voice.[1]

> "When our convictions are yielded to God completely, He is able to give Himself to us in all His fullness. Until that is so, He cannot entrust us. Unfortunately, we often miss the joy and strength of our Christianity. The reason is simple; when we withhold ourselves from Jesus, we make it impossible for Him to give Himself to us in the fullness of His grace and truth."
>
> Andrew Murray

Without Him in our lives, we are simply average. All that is good within us comes from the Father and so we can agree that we desperately need Him more each day.

As mentioned earlier, the area where we most commonly withhold ourselves from God is the area of prayer. We should not be surprised that the enemy consistently targets that area of our lives. He knows the net results if he succeeds. Prayer is the lifeline of the Christian. Without active and purposeful communication with God, we are comatose and ineffective.

That is why most of us are running on empty and are rendered feeble and ineffective in our roles as leaders. We cannot continue walking like this a minute longer. We must determine to end this now - yes, this very minute.

Some of you may think that I am overreacting. To those of you who are thinking in that vein, I ask you this, "How important is your eternity? How important is the eternal destination of those whom you are called to lead or reach?"

I urge you to reconsider the value that you may have attributed to this matter up to this moment. Raise the stakes and move in the direction that God is placing before you. When we don't pray regularly and engage in dialogue with the Father, we are declaring harsh statements to the heavens. In short, you are stating that you are enough and that you don't need His intervention and leading. Now, you and I know that we desperately need Him. However, following are three examples of statements we declare when we omit prayer from our lives:

1. Prayerlessness is a declaration of self-sufficiency.

Remember as a kid telling your parents, "I got this…" Everything in you declared that you were grown and ready to handle whatever was before you. However, your parents knew better. To refuse to take your needs and concerns to God is a similar declaration of self-sufficiency. We are saying to Him, "Thanks God, but I don't need You. I'll work it out." Only after worry and failure do we realize that our sufficiency is in God. D. L. Moody expressed a similar sentiment when he said, "To suppose that whatever God requires of us that we have power of ourselves to do, is to make the cross and grace of Jesus Christ of none effect."

Manasseh was Judah's most wicked king. He made Jerusalem
"...*do more evil than the nations whom the LORD destroyed*".[2] He was
self-sufficient. He believed that he did not need God; he ran his
own life. But when the Assyrians took Manasseh captive to Baby-
lon, he discovered he was not as self-sufficient as he thought.[3]
Like Manasseh, we often need a rude awakening before we open
our eyes and come to a place of realization that God is our only
true source.

In John 15:5, we are reminded, "*Without God, we can do nothing.*" Not spending time with God in prayer demonstrates that we
think we can handle things on our own. Spending time with Him
in prayer shows that we are dependent on Him. But that is not
all! He also shows us His provision and capacity to see us through
all situations. That is where we belong: complete reliance on the
God who has never failed. Apart from Him we can do nothing.[4]

**2. Prayerlessness is a refusal to exercise a blood-
purchased honor.**

When Jesus went to the cross, suffered and died, the veil of
the temple was ripped in two. This signified there would never
again be anything keeping man out of God's presence when we
come to Him through Jesus. If we do not spend time with God in
prayer, we neglect a divine privilege. When we consistently spend
time with the Father in prayer we are taking full advantage of
this great privilege of entering God's presence. Take a moment to
meditate on how amazing this is for you and me. We have access
to the King of kings and Lord of lords. Let's utilize this precious
privilege purchased for us on Calvary. Prayerlessness is a cruel
refusal to accept a purchased privilege.[5] Christ's death opened
the way for us to enter into fellowship with the Father in a
manner unlike ever before in human history. This has been God's
desire since the beginning, and through the cross it was finally
made possible. Do not waste this precious gift.

3. Prayerlessness is sin against a holy God.

In Scripture, we see many examples of where we are instructed and even commanded to pray. This is not only the lifeline of a leader and a believer, but also an expression of obedience to a holy God. Here are two verses that will help us see this imperative:

1 Thessalonians 5:17 tells us to,

> *"Rejoice always, pray continually, give thanks in all circumstances; for this is God's will for you [us] in Christ Jesus."*

Then in Luke 18:1 we read,

> *"Then Jesus told his disciples a parable to show them that they should always pray and not give up."*

We are commanded to pray. Failure to pray is disobedience. Have you ever considered this truth? If you do have a consistent prayer life you should be encouraged that you are obeying God. The Prophet Samuel recognized that prayerlessness was sin against a holy God.

> *"Moreover, as for me, far be it from me that I should sin against the Lord by ceasing to pray for you…"*
>
> 1 Samuel 12:23

The enemy will try to stop you from praying, or even entice you to do life on your own; this is a temptation that began in the Garden of Eden. That is not God's design. We are to go to the Lord with our hearts open and our ears attuned to His voice. When we pray, He listens and He also speaks.

So, what happens when we do live a lifestyle of prayer? Here is a short list of some truths:

1. God's divine hand will move freely.
2. God will accomplish great things through us, His vessels.
3. God will move by His Spirit, through us, to glorify Himself.

When we pray, we tap into the endless source of power and anointing from heaven. The process of prayer represents the inexhaustible source that comes from God. He will provide power, presence and anointing to accomplish His will for our lives. This concept is captured in Zechariah 4:6-7, where the Lord says,

> "Not by might nor by power, but by My Spirit,
> says the Lord of hosts."

The ideal setting to experience God's Spirit is in the act of prayer. This again serves to remind us why the enemy of our souls does all he can to distract us from that spiritual discipline. Yet many of us continue to operate on an empty tank. More than ever before in the history of mankind, we must enter into His presence in prayer to be filled by His power, His Spirit and His anointing. Then we will experience His best, and finish the work He's called us to since before time. Anything less will simply fall short and lead us to a place of despair and desperation.

REFLECTION

What has been the greatest obstacle to your time of prayer and devotions with the Lord? How have you or will you overcome that?

_____

_____

_____

_____

_____

_____

_____

_____

_____

_____

What Scripture inspires you to spend time before the Lord?

_____

_____

_____

_____

_____

_____

_____

_____

_____

_____

If prayer remains elusive in your life, would you consider an accountability partner? This person would pray with you and hold you accountable to a regular pattern of prayer. Identify that person and write their name here: _____.

---

1. Read 1 Kings 19:11-13
2. Chron. 33:9
3. 2 Chron. 33:12-13
4. John 15:5
5. Hebrews 10:19-23

8

Where Feet May Fail

"God is looking for those with whom He can do the impossible— what a pity that we plan only the things that we can do by ourselves."
— A. W. Tozer

L et's begin this chapter by reading Matthew 14:22-33:

Immediately Jesus made the disciples get into the boat and go on ahead of him to the other side, while he dismissed the crowd. After he had dismissed them, he went up on a mountainside by himself to pray. Later that night, he was there alone, and the boat was already a considerable distance from land, buffeted by the waves because the wind was against it. Shortly before dawn Jesus went out to them, walking on the lake. When the

disciples saw him walking on the lake, they were
terrified.
"It's a ghost," they said, and cried out in fear.
But Jesus immediately said to them: "Take courage! It is I.
Don't be afraid."
"Lord, if it's you," Peter replied, "tell me to come to you on
the water."¹
"Come," he said. Then Peter got down out of the boat,
walked on the water and came toward Jesus. But when
he saw the wind, he was afraid and, beginning to sink,
cried out, "Lord, save me!"
Immediately Jesus reached out his hand and caught him.
"You of little faith," he said, "why did you doubt?"²
And when they climbed into the boat, the wind died
down. Then those who were in the boat worshiped him,
saying, "Truly you are the Son of God."

In his book, *"Three Steps Forward, Two Steps Back,"* Chuck Swindoll tells a story about a farmer who wanted to impress his hunting buddies. So, he went out and bought the smartest, most expensive hunting dog he could find. He trained this dog to do amazing things – things no other dog on earth could do. Then he invited his neighbors to go duck hunting with him. After a long patient wait in the boat a group of ducks flew over and the hunters shot a few of them down. Several ducks fell in the water.

The farmer looked at the dog and said, "Go get 'em!" The dog leaped out of the boat, walked on the water, and picked up a bird and returned to the boat. As soon as he dropped the duck in the boat he trotted off across the water again and grabbed another duck and brought it back to the boat.

The owner swelled with pride as his dog walked across the water and retrieved each of the birds one by one. Smugly, he looked at one of his buddies and asked, "Do you notice anything unusual about my dog?" One of them sat back and rubbed his chin and thought about it for a little while and finally said, "Yeah, come to think of it, I do! That stupid dog of yours doesn't know how to swim does he?"

Go ahead and it's okay to chuckle. You know this was a good one! The funny (or ironic) thing about this simple illustration is that many people give this story about Peter walking on water a similar reaction.

Rather than recognizing that he was the only disciple who stepped out of the boat – he's often criticized for his apparent "lack of faith." However, if we take a moment, we can observe that he was the only one willing to take the risk – while the eleven other Disciples sat in the boat content in their perceived safety as spectators.

Have you ever played the role of one of the eleven Disciples? I know I have taken on that role many times during my journey. I have watched from the sideline or safety of the boat once too many times. If you have also, you are in good company. This is not the moment to beat yourself with guilt and condemnation. It is simply an opportunity for honest assessment and surrender. Remember this, self-assessment without surrender becomes a burden - one you were never meant to carry. With that in mind, let us take a closer look at this topic.

The truth of the matter is that God will often call us to a place and purpose greater than our abilities, intelligence and even courage. A place "where feet may fail." As we saw in this portion of Scripture, our friend Peter saw something and desired it – even though in his heart and mind, he knew it was not possible in the natural. The other men saw the same thing as Peter, but they were gripped by fear and therefore remained paralyzed by their limitations.

When I teach, I always like to explore the balance and synergy between Old and New Testaments. Let's take this conversation and look at a similar scenario in the Old Testament. The story that best falls into this discussion is found in the book of Numbers chapter thirteen. This well-known story details the exploits of twelve men; they were spies who were sent by Moses into Canaan to secretly explore the land. As in our New Testament story, all of the spies saw the land flowing with milk and honey. There was no argument or discrepancy on that point. Unfortunately, most of the spies chose to focus on the might and size of the inhabitants of the land. They did the same thing as the eleven men in the boat who chose to focus on the rough waves; overlooking Jesus, the Messiah, walking on the water. The exception to this case was Joshua and Caleb. Like Peter, they chose to see the potential before them, while not ignoring the realities of the challenge around them:

> *"Then Caleb silenced the people before Moses and said,*
> *"We should go up and take possession of the land, for*
> *we can certainly do it."*
>
> Numbers 13:30

The "majority report" said no, but two men said yes! Sadly, most leaders today will shrink back when confronted by the wide expanse of uncharted waters or threatening giants. Those leaders will never experience the pleasure and miracle of walking on water or conquering uncharted lands. They will never experience the power of God's rescuing hands when they fail in their pursuit of the miraculous. That is why God is seeking leaders, men and women, who possess the bodacious courage of Caleb, Joshua and the unrelenting determination of Peter. That said, God is not looking for perfection; but rather, those who are willing to dream and break through barriers.

Are you living with dormant dreams, untapped potential, amazing yet unrealized purpose? I am sure that there are many who fall into that category. You have allowed fear to keep you in your proverbial boat or outside of the territory that God has called you to conquer.

Peter was afraid just like the other men. But he pressed through his fear in order to experience the supernatural. He chose not to live with the regret of "What if..." I am sure that Joshua and Caleb had to choose to believe God as they reported back to Moses. This position of belief against the odds is a supernatural experience and one that requires intentionality. So how do we get there, John? I am glad you asked!

There are three things that I want you to consider for yourself and those whom you lead at home, in ministry, and even in your business. As you do this, I challenge you to take inventory of your journey and allow the Lord to speak into those areas that require complete surrender. Now let us examine and focus on three actions taken by Peter:

1. "Lord if it is you... tell me to come to you on the water."

Peter could have uttered the words, "Why, Lord?!" But he saw something that he wanted; something that moved him to consider the impossible. Peter found his purpose and identity in Christ, and he was compelled to pursue that, even if it meant walking on water. How crazy is that? Yet this is what God requires of us.

Like Peter, we must always be ready to seek Him, talk to Him, ask Him for His will and know His heart. Understand that the ability to walk on water, experiencing the supernatural, is not found within you but in Christ.

"I can do all things through Christ who strengthens me."

Philippians 4:13

The waves will often reveal the fiber of our character and knowledge of an all-powerful God. Someone once said, *"Who you believe God to be is the single most important factor of your life. High views of God lead to high and holy living. Low views of God lead to low and based living."*[3] Similarly, Hudson Taylor, the great missionary, once wrote, *"All God's giants have been weak men who did great things for God because they reckoned on His being with them."*

So today, God is telling you, *"I am with you."* He is also telling you to fix your heart to trust in Him. Then you will experience all that he has promised in Scripture. All that God has made available through the plan of redemption is yours to have. But you must settle that issue in your own heart and know that His power and promises are not just for a chosen few, but also for all who believe.

2. "Then Peter got down out of the boat, walked on water and came toward Jesus..."

We have all heard the saying, "Put your money where your mouth is..." It is one thing to talk about your dreams and purpose; it is a completely different thing to act on them. Too many leaders spend their entire lives expressing what they will one day do to solve an issue, create an opportunity or help a community. Day after day, they think about it and talk about it, yet nothing happens.

This is a cycle that is often driven by fear, insecurity and complacency. None of those qualities promote vision nor invite Jesus into the equation. I must confess that I wasted many years because of fear and insecurities. I focused my eyes on the waves, rather than on Jesus. Today, my eyes are fixed on Jesus, as the source of my hope, purpose and future. No more wasted time.

We can all agree that what Peter did was absolutely outrageous, ridiculous and altogether insane! However, when Jesus said, "come," Peter obeyed. Have you heard the voice of God in your heart saying, "Come. Follow me." Or "Dare to believe?"

The problem is that when we hear God speak, it rarely makes sense in the natural. His directives always depend on His power so that He receives glory. That will undoubtedly thrust us into the realm of the supernatural. This is rarely a place of comfort. This is the place where the million-dollar question comes to the surface: "What if I step out of the boat and sink?" That is the number one dream and purpose killer. Yet, it is a fair question! So, let's address that issue.

3. He [Peter] "cried out, Lord, save me!"

Why did Peter exclaim those words? The answer is simple; he was sinking! His attempt to walk on water started out great, but clearly did not end well. So, did he fail? Well to be honest, yes, in one sense he did fail. His faith did give way - he couldn't keep his eyes locked on Jesus. He allowed himself to become distracted. He sank - He failed. Before you think that I am being tough on Peter, allow me to expand on this theme a bit further. There were eleven bigger failures in the boat. They failed privately; they failed quietly, and their failure by and large has gone un-criticized. Only poor Peter experienced the shame of public failure. But on the other hand, Peter is the only one who knew the glory of walking on the water. He did not allow his fear to keep him back.

Did you know that the strongest faith and the greatest courage each share a common ingredient? They each contain an element of fear. It is that fear that often becomes the launching pad for great achievements and bold stances on God's promises. Someone once said, "Just because you feel fear doesn't mean you can't do it. *Do it afraid!*" This sentiment is bolstered by the Scripture found in Mark 9:24 where the father of an ill child demonstrates that those who can say, "Lord, I believe;" must also say, Lord, "help my unbelief."

When "sinking" days come around, reach for His hand. That takes as much faith as believing that He can cause you to walk on water. Moreover, keep in mind that He can rescue you from the waves. With that in mind, is there really a risk in stepping out of the boat? Following are several reminders from Scripture that will help you move onto the waters and into your promise:

"You didn't choose me, I chose you [to live out that dream, that purpose, that calling]" so you must go in the confidence that God has us covered and will guide and protect us all the days of our lives."

John 15:16

"But he said to me, "My grace is sufficient for you, for my power is made perfect in weakness."

2 Corinthians 12:9-10

"For it is God who works in you to will and to act in order to fulfill his good purpose."

Philippians 2:13

"The one who calls you is faithful, and he will do it."

1 Thessalonians 5:24

Last but not least, I leave you with Hebrews 13:20-21, my prayer for you today:

"And now may the God of peace, who brought

again from the dead our Lord Jesus, equip you
with all you need for doing his will. May he
who became the great Shepherd of the sheep
by an everlasting agreement between God and
you, signed with his blood, produce in you
through the power of Christ all that is pleasing
to him. To him be glory forever and ever.
Amen."

Franklin D. Roosevelt once said, "It is common sense to take
a method and try it. If it fails, admit it frankly. But above all, try
something!" Choosing not to try something because you desire to
be secure results in apathy and failure to lead. The temptation of
self-preservation always leads to faithless and empty lives. With
that in mind, and as we come to the close of this chapter, I want
to challenge you to go ahead and mobilize your faith. Find the
time in the days ahead to step out of your boat and run to the
shoreline of your promised territory.

REFLECTION

Can you describe the place where God is calling you that will require audacious faith?

_____

_____

_____

_____

_____

_____

_____

_____

_____

_____

_____

What has stopped you thus far from achieving your dream, and your purpose?

_____

_____

_____

_____

_____

_____

_____

_____

_____

Describe the first three steps of your action plan.

_____

_____

_____

_____

_____

_____

_____

_____

_____

_____

_____

_____

_____

_____

_____

_____

_____

_____

_____

1. Weird request! Most would have asked, "if it is you, tell me something that only you would know about me..."
2. Most of my life, I imagined Christ saying these words with a stern voice and frustrated look on his face." Today, I imagine him saying those words with a loving voice and a loving grin on his face...
3. Ligonier Ministries, 2019

9

Leading Through
Insurmountable Crisis

*"You're not made in a crisis — you're revealed. When you squeeze an orange
— you get orange juice. When you squeeze a lemon — you get lemon juice.
When a human being gets squeezed — you get what
is inside — positive or negative."*
— *Jack Kinder*

We all witnessed a dreadful phenomenon that began in China during the fall of 2019, then it eventually touched the entire globe at the onset of 2020. We know this crisis as the COVID-19 pandemic. The unimaginable, and sadly, unexpected rampage against life has been nothing short of a horror movie. This experience will mark every man and woman on this planet for decades and shape our thoughts and actions for generations to come. We will continue to change over time in an effort to avoid a repeat performance. This will be the new challenge for leaders across all sectors in the years and perhaps decades to follow.

Suffice it to say that this global event will be likened to an earlier life-changing event that we call: 9/11. While the global effects of 9/11 were quite different, it nonetheless changed our way of life and the fiber of each person who lived through the events of September 11th, 2001. Everyone remembers where they were when the planes hit the two towers of the World Trade Center in New York City and the Pentagon.

Where were you? As for me, I was sitting outside of my home office watching the news of an apparent "plane accident," when right before my eyes, another plane struck the second tower. In that moment, I knew that the crash was not an accident; it was an attack on the United States. In an instant, I was changed. My sense of safety was immediately taken away. Since I grew up around the towers in lower Manhattan, my entire life flashed right before my eyes. I realized that my city, and my memories would be forever tainted by this catastrophic event. A city and a nation would be indelibly changed and propelled into a new era... We were transmuted into a reality where safety from foreign enemies was no longer guaranteed. Our concept of travel, business and even our global vernacular was changed, never to return.

The generation that witnessed and lived through that horrific event would be painfully marked by that day. Over the course of several days, and weeks, we began to pull through as a nation - united and stronger than ever. However, we emerged as a different people. Though filled with uncertainty and fear for my loved ones, I had to remain focused as a leader and continue serving the people around me. There was no time to waste.

So how does one lead through times like these, when the world seems to be at the brink of implosion and everyone is in the throes of chaos? Who are you, and who am I to lead? This dilemma is magnified by the fact that when things fall into absolute pandemonium, you as a leader are also in the heat of the moment, feeling the crush and pain, just like everyone else.

What is the right thing to do? What is the right thing to say? The truth of the matter is that there are many viable answers to these questions. However, I want to focus on two simple thoughts that I found to be weighty and true during the early days of the COVID-19 crisis; the most difficult experience of my lifetime.

Most leaders immediately turn to and reach for "wisdom" when faced with crisis. There is nothing wrong with that. As a matter of fact, it's a good response to crisis. However, I want to challenge you as a leader to keep the following principle in mind: during seasons of great crisis, suffering and pain, the people you lead will not initially look for your wisdom as much as they will look for your love and empathy. They want to first know that you understand their pain. They will have an innate demand to know that you are in the boat with them and that you are leading from a place of camaraderie. If you are leading a team during crisis, they will need to see this in you so that they may also project the same for those they lead. Your church, ministry or team needs to know that you sincerely care. They need to see you close, not from afar and disconnected from their reality. This is to be considered a point of strength, not weakness.

A leader who is able to convey love through his or her gifts and efforts is one who is willing to go deeper and farther than any strategist who relies solely on facts and figures. I witnessed this during the COVID-19 pandemic. Several mayors, governors and other elected officials netted our attention because of their exposure to media and of course the cities they led. Some were negative, disconnected and even defensive and consumed with transfer of blame on other leaders. Conversely, other leaders shared similar grim facts, but infused hope and reliable information that provided a sound perspective. The healthy leaders provided their constituents with facts and tools to navigate white waters. They also provided emotional and personal messages that allowed the conversation to remain humane and heartfelt. They reminded their audience that they too were in this crisis and that together, "we" would come through somehow.

Leaders who make the effort to convey that they care in the midst of crisis will be remembered for that very reason. On the other hand, those leaders who are negative and solely fixed on survival and grim facts, will also be remembered for that reason. The difference between these two examples is quite clear. As a result the longevity of their careers will be directly impacted. People want to follow smart, wise and gifted leaders, but they also need to know that there is a heart in that leader. This reminds me of a quote by Carl W. Buchner – "People may not remember exactly what you did, or what you said, but they will always remember how you made them feel."

I found these wonderful attributes in effect, in the life and leadership of Franklin Graham during the early months of the Covid-19 pandemic. During the onset of this crisis, he was perfectly positioned by God as the leader of two amazing organizations. He was the head of the Billy Graham Evangelistic Association (BGEA) and also head of Samaritan's Purse. The first is an organization dedicated to the proclamation of the Gospel, by all means possible. The second organization is known worldwide for its top-shelf humanitarian services. So as this pandemic sunk its teeth into this nation and beyond our borders, Franklin Graham moved into position and mobilized his teams. His initial response was to share his concern, compassion and most importantly God's love. He launched a 24-hour prayer line through BGEA that was staffed with volunteers, from both organizations, who were able to pray for, and counsel over 100,000 people during the initial weeks of operation. That number grew exponentially over the course of weeks and months. I had the pleasure of volunteering for this endeavor and personally experienced the impact of passionate leadership and the power of prayer during these weeks of outreach.

In addition, Franklin Graham employed his leadership wisdom and years of experience to mobilize Samaritan's Purse medical teams in Milan, Italy and in New York City. Each medical operation was able to treat approximately 80 critical Covid patients at any given time. This, again, was an example of leadership, love and wisdom in action during crisis. You may not be Franklin Graham or the leader of any other major ministry but you serve the same God as Franklin. Therefore, you too have access to God's infinite love and wisdom in the midst of crisis.

We see this real-world example and the overarching principle given to us in the book of Romans[1], as it instructs us to *"Rejoice with those who rejoice; mourn with those who mourn."* There is something about the leader who can effectively achieve this in the context of those whom he or she serves. This Scripture conveys a subtle message of closeness and understanding, and it is there to compel us to remain near to those whom we lead. This doesn't mean that you sit and emotionally cradle every person under you. You may be the leader of a large team or ministry, so clearly that may not be a viable option for you. Yet, your heartfelt words and deeds can cause those around you to feel your empathy, almost in tangible form. Achieving this quality in your leadership role will become a significant subsidy to your life's work.

You see; acquiring this attribute will further align you with the greatest leader to ever grace this planet. Who is that you ask? It is my genuine belief that the greatest leader to ever grace this planet was Jesus. Yes, that is quite the statement if you don't know Him as the Son of God. So, let's take a closer look at my statement solely from a leadership perspective.

We know the likes of men like Socrates, Mahatma Gandhi, George Washington and Winston Churchill, to name a few. As an aggregate, these men produced approximately a century's worth of influence and teaching during their combined years of leadership. They also inspired, educated and led countless apprentices during their respective vocations. While each man had noteworthy influence on culture, government, and other arenas – there were clear margins to their overall impact when compared to Jesus' leadership.

Jesus on the other hand only led for three short years and directly mentored a small group of twelve men. As for Jesus' travels, many scholars say that the furthest he traveled during his ministry was only a few hundred miles from his hometown. Nevertheless, He defeated death, transformed the world, influenced history, and even governments. What's more, his name currently inspires over two billion Christians across this great planet. Yes, he is inarguably the greatest leader to ever live. But wait, there's more! If Jesus, whom we can agree was the greatest leader ever to live, was able to empathize and lead with his heart, who are we to shy away from that level of authenticity?

One of my favorite examples of this is found in John 11:35. This is the shortest verse in the Bible, yet it is one of the most profound in the New Testament. The verse tells us that *"Jesus wept"* when He was presented at the scene of Lazarus' death. The magnitude of that moment moved him to tears. It is important to note that this was not a private event, but public! There was no attempt on His part to hide his emotions. Jesus felt for those impacted by the death of Lazarus and he was not afraid to show it.

From this place of compassion and empathy, we witness one of the greatest miracles performed by Jesus. You too can experience great miracles when love and empathy for others are present and mobilized in your life and ministry.

Now, I would be remiss if I stopped here and said nothing about the importance of bringing the balance of wisdom and passion into your leadership role. Keep in mind that you will always employ both as a leader; they are not mutually exclusive. However, some situations may call on one into a lead role, while the other plays a supporting role. For example, when I work out with weights in a gym, I use my entire body for balance. I also need my entire body engaged to generate the necessary momentum and strength to move the weights for multiple repetitions. With that said, when I am curling dumbbells, I primarily use my biceps in that exercise. However, most other muscles remain engaged in a supportive role to ensure that my body is in balance and remains injury free. So with that idea in mind, wisdom and passion can become the ideal synthesis for success when employed in balance and order. So how many cups of wisdom should I add, and how many tablespoons of passion should I sprinkle into a given situation? Don't sweat it; God will show you in that moment as you remain positioned close to His heart.

All you must do is remain cognizant that you will have to employ wisdom during seasons of great crisis. This is actually an important stewardship principle. Leaders must lead in balance and integrity of heart. So, while you are leading in love and connecting with those you lead, you must also have a plan. You must operate in the wisdom and leading of the Holy Spirit. During times of great crisis, you will be called to lead through uncharted and rough white waters. While you will be expected to have answers, you will never have all the answers. There will be many moments, especially in crisis, when you will also have to tap into your team and even uncover rare gems among them. If you read through the Gospels, you will see this truth come to life as you study the relationship between Jesus and His Disciples.[2]

Someone once said that leaders require great cerebral dexterity to discover what others really believe. What wise people think and believe could help you succeed as a leader. Conversely, what fools think and say could cost you dearly. Only a leader who possesses wisdom will also have the know-how and wherewithal to unearth helpful strategies and ideas out of others.

My prayer for you as a leader is that God would give you the eyes to see who is on your team, and around you during your toughest seasons. This will require you to actively and prayerfully listen and observe. As you do this, you will find the assets and liabilities that exist on your team. We see this beautifully played out in the Gospels as Jesus applied great wisdom in His dealings with Peter, who had a character issue, and with Judas, who had a heart issue. Jesus loved each of them equally, but in dealing with them, He was able to discern who was teachable and who was obstinate. As you know, Peter went on to be one of the founding fathers of the church, while Judas met his own demise, as the weight of his betrayal was too much to endure.

This leadership concept is also presented in Proverbs 20:5, where we learn that the *"Counsel in the heart of man is like deep water; but a man of understanding will draw it out."* This is one of the greatest tasks of a leader in times of crisis.

The illustration in the Scripture above presents a deep well, where the water lies far below the surface of the ground. In order to obtain the water, significant ingenuity and hard work must be employed to reach down to retrieve the water. Only a creative and industrious leader will identify the means and put forth the effort. Most will look elsewhere for easier waters. Not you!

When you begin to lead during a season of great challenge and difficulty (and you will), I pray that God will give you the tenacity and vigor to unearth the gold that exists in the lives of those around you. Do not fear the process. Do not avoid the hard work and difficult conversations. Through these watershed moments, your leadership will be fortified, just as steel in the heat of a refiner's furnace. You will be purified and prepared for use by the King of heaven and earth.

Psalm 66:10-12: "For You have tried us, O God; You have refined us as silver is refined. You brought us into the net; You laid an oppressive burden upon our loins. You made men ride over our heads; We went through fire and through water, Yet You brought us out into a place of abundance."

As you begin to tap into the resources in the members of your team, some may fear sharing their talents and opinions with you, their leader, even if they've known you for years. However, the

Holy Spirit will give you the grace to encourage them to a place of trust and honesty.

As you stretch your team and tap into their wells, there may be some who may carry tainted motivations as a result of fear, scars and insecurities carried from past experiences. As you remain close to God, He will reveal these things to you, give you discernment, and will position you to show grace in correction and redirection. That is what Jesus did with His Disciples, namely Peter, and we all know how effective they were in turning the world upside down for His glory.

He "appointed twelve, that they might be with him and that he might send them out to preach..."

Mark 3:14 (NKJV)

REFLECTION

What has been your greatest leadership crisis? How did you influence your team, church, or organization during the crisis?

_____

_____

_____

_____

_____

_____

_____

_____

_____

_____

_____

Can you think of a crisis where you buckled under the pressure? How did you recover? What lesson did you learn from your experience?

_____

_____

_____

_____

_____

_____

_____

_____

How has God used crisis to grow you as a Christian and leader?

_____

_____

_____

_____

_____

_____

_____

_____

_____

_____

_____

_____

_____

_____

_____

_____

_____

_____

_____

_____

_____

_____

_____

_____

_____

1. Romans 12:15
2. Luke 10

10

The Climber's Prayer

*"When Jesus saw his ministry drawing huge crowds, he climbed a hillside.
Those who were apprenticed to him, the committed, climbed with him.
Arriving at a quiet place, he sat down and taught his climbing companions."*
– Matthew 5:1-2 (MSG)

I recently learned that there is such a thing as a Rock Climber's Prayer that goes like this: "Dear Lord, I realize I could be better, and do better, and I'll get back to that in a moment, but right now I've got a problem. I'm hanging on to a little nubbin of rock, not sure I'm going to be able to make the next move. My knees are shaking, my arms are tired, and falling is going to hurt. A lot. Dear Lord, here's the deal; help me stretch to make this move, get me to the top safe and sound, and I'm all yours; every Sunday, and twice on Easter. Forever."

I chuckled when I initially read this prayer. It seemed silly, but in many ways, some parts were quite relatable. It was at this moment, that I realized that every climber should engage with Jesus in an intimate exchange prior to embarking on a life-changing climb. All climbers should sit at His feet and learn what He has to say specifically to that unique endeavor of life. The climber should leave all excess baggage at the foot of the mountain and allow Jesus to remove unnecessary weights and encumbrances. This is also where you (as the climber) surrender all to Him and entrust your ascent to His faithful teaching and guidance. This is when the climb truly commences.

With that said, I thought that there could be no other way to close this book and journey (with you) than with a time of prayer. The prayer that I shared at the beginning of this chapter was in jest; however, the prayer that we are about to partake of is where our ascension to the summit begins. So with no further ado, I believe it is time to pray.

Here is how we will do this. Below is a prayer that you and I will declare as we bring our time together to a close. Once you are done, take a moment to express your deepest thoughts and sentiments to God. Tell Him how you feel; what you dread; what you need; and lastly, share whatever else is on your heart. When you are through speaking to Him and waiting on Him, then I would submit that you take time to write down your reflections and what you believe He has deposited into your heart. Okay, now let us pray:

"Jesus, today, I receive the fullness of the call that you have placed on my life. I repent of all my sins, the many times that I doubted you, and those moments when I quietly resigned. I declare this day that I will no longer quit; I will not settle for less than what you have called me to. Starting today, I will become a steadfast climber. I will fulfill the call on my life. I will reach the summit, and give you all glory and honor. I wholeheartedly receive the victory that you purchased on the cross of Calvary. Amen!"

REFLECTION

Sources

Ardley, Neil. (Page 38) *Dictionary of Science: 2000 Key Words Arranged Thematically.* London: Dorling Kindersley, 1994: 57

Absolute Surrender by Andrew Murray (1828-1917) First published in 1895. This edition, Chicago: Moody Press

Holy Bible: The New King James Version. 1982. Nashville: Thomas Nelson.

https://www.govexec.com/management/2014/04/8-reasons-small-teams-work-better/82804/

Jewish New Testament Publications, Jerusalem, 1989

"Matthew Henry Complete Bible Commentary Online." *Bible Study Tools*, Salem Web Network, www.biblestudytools.com/commentaries/matthew-henry-complete/.

NIV Study Bible. Kenneth L. Barker, gen. ed. 10th anniversary ed. Grand Rapids, MI: Zondervan, 1995. Print.

Roger Nicole, *The Expositor's Bible Commentary*, Zondervan, Grand Rapids, 1979, Vol. I, p. 617

Swindoll, Charles R.. (1980). *Three steps forward, two steps back : persevering through pressure* . Nashville: Thomas Nelson Publisher.

Tyndale House Publishers. (2004). Holy Bible: New Living Translation. Wheaton, Ill: Tyndale House Publishers.

Webster; https://www.merriam-webster.com/ dictionary/con%20game

Westminster Assembly, Kelly, D. F., Rollinson, P. B., & Marsh, F. T. (1986). The Westminster Shorter catechism in modern English. Phillipsburg, N.J: Presbyterian and Reformed Pub. Co.

About the Author

John Rivera is a native New Yorker. He was raised in a Christian home and began his personal journey with the Lord at a young age. Ministry entered his life shortly after his sixteenth birthday and soon became his lifelong passion.

He began working in youth ministry during the late 1980's and continued serving in New York and New Jersey to this day. Over the years, the Lord has granted John the opportunity to also serve in a variety of leadership positions in local churches and organizations. Some of those roles included that of deacon, teacher, ministry leader, and board member.

John has an extensive background as a trainer and consultant in organizational and leadership development. Since 1995, John has helped many churches and nonprofit organizations grow, define their vision and execute in excellence. He served as

Director of Ministry Relations for a New York Christian radio station over a period of four years. In that role, he used his experience and knowledge to help churches throughout the New York tri-state area reach beyond their four walls and experience ministry at a higher level. To achieve this, John worked with Pastors to create strategies that allowed them to mobilize their congregations around a clear vision and most importantly, the Great Commission. He has often expressed that "there is no greater satisfaction, than seeing the lost introduced to a loving Savior and the redeemed living their God-ordained purpose."

John earned a bachelor's degree in Communication Arts from William Paterson University of NJ. He graduated Summa Cum Laude and was the sole recipient of the celebrated "Excellence In Interpersonal Communication Theory Award."

Today John continues to use his years of experience to assist area ministries and organizations with their development needs through his consulting practice that was formed in 2012 for the exclusive purpose of *encouraging, equipping and empowering* organizations to accomplish their mission as well as grow their impact and footprint. The focus of his consulting work is simple: Solving Problems & Adding Value (SPAV). This is John's view of his role in the lives of people and organizations. He believes that this concept represents the balance that should exist in every leader's life. All leaders must present a balanced effort between activities that solve problems and those that add value. If one leans too much in one direction, then there will be imbalance in the leader's life and the organization. John loves his role as a coach to organizational leaders. As such, he strongly believes that individuals can all rise to a higher level of excellence as they pursue their purpose and mission in life.

In addition to his many roles in the Christian and business communities, John is husband to the love of his life, Naomi Rivera. He is also the proud father of two amazing sons: Zachary

John and Matthew Ryan. The Rivera's reside in Northern New Jersey.

To learn more about John's consulting practice and ministry work, please send your inquiry to:

John Rivera
Vive Consulting Group, LLC
Jrivera.vive@gmail.com

VIVE CONSULTING

Made in the USA
Coppell, TX
15 January 2022